T0051816

The Heart of the Universe

the Heart *of the* Universe

exploring the Heart Sutra

by Mu Soeng

Wisdom Publications

Wisdom Publications
199 Elm Street
Somerville MA 02144 USA
www.wisdompubs.org

Library of Congress Cataloging-in-Publication Data
Mu, Soeng.
 The heart of the universe : exploring the Heart Sutra / by Mu Soeng.
    p. cm.
 Includes bibliographical references.
 ISBN 0-86171-574-8 (pbk. : alk. paper)
 1. Tripiṭaka. Sūtrapiṭaka. Prajñāpāramitā. Hṛdaya—Commentaries. I. Title.
 BQ1967.M8 2010
 294.3'85—dc22
                        2009044740

14 13 12 11 10
5 4 3 2 1

Cover design by Phil Pascuzzo. Interior design by TLLC. Set in Diacritical Garamond Pro 11.5/15.5.

Wisdom Publications' books are printed on acid-free paper and meet the guidelines for permanence and durability of the Production Guidelines for Book Longevity of the Council on Library Resources.

Printed in the United States of America.

This book was produced with environmental mindfulness. We have elected to print this title on 30% PCW recycled paper. As a result, we have saved the following resources: 27 trees, 4 million BTUs of energy, 1,088 lbs. of greenhouse gases, 5,239 gallons of water, and 318 lbs. of solid waste. For more information, please visit our website, www.wisdompubs.org. This paper is also FSC certified. For more information, please visit www.fscus.org.

Table of Contents

Introduction

At the heart of each of us, whatever our imperfections, there exists
a silent pulse of perfect rhythm, a complex of wave-forms and res-
onances, which is absolutely individual and unique, and yet which
connects us to everything in the universe. The act of getting in
touch with this pulse can transform our personal experience and
in some way alter the world around us.

—George Leonard[1]

The convergence between science and mysticism, between
Eastern thought and Western pragmatism and empiricism,
and the consequent emergence of a new paradigm in recent times, offers
a renewed hope that we can transform ourselves and the world around
us. The dangers of failing to do so are readily apparent, mostly in the
near destruction of the ecological system of the planet. There are many
tools of transformation, but the only place where transformation really
takes place is in the human heart. The ancient traditions of the East have
sought to understand the nature of reality within one's own heart. It is
not an accident that the Chinese word *hsin* stands for heart-mind, rather
than just one of those two concepts. In the Eastern way of looking at
things, the thinking-feeling process is a unified field, in contrast to
Cartesian dualism and Western science's separation of mind and body.
The Buddha spoke of *nama-rupa* (mind-body) as a continuum.
Human experience has shown that the heart-mind, being deeply conditioned, is not an easy place for conflicts to be resolved. Deep meditative
insights are just as difficult to be accepted by our conditioned emotional

frameworks as the findings of contemporary scientific research. We humans are still guided deeply, perhaps unconsciously, by our emotions, despite our claims to be rational beings. This was brought out most vividly in the intense emotional and even existential crisis that the pioneers of quantum physics (the post-Einsteinian branch of physics that deals with the molecular structure of organisms at the subatomic or the quantum level) underwent before they could accept the intellectual findings of their own experiments. Einstein reportedly said that "God does not play dice with the universe" on the findings of randomness in quantum mechanics and the uncertainty it generated. To accept that the universe is random or that uncertainty is its prime operating principle requires a huge emotional adjustment.

The Heart Sutra, an ancient scripture from the Mahayana wisdom school of Buddhism, offers us insight into the nature of an ultimate reality through intuitive wisdom. The spaciousness of this insight allows the heart to beat in its naturalness, beyond disputations and ideological arguments. Now that quantum physics has found some interesting parallels to the basic insights of the Heart Sutra, perhaps the intellectual and the intuitive can meet.

Although this commentary intends to view the insights of Mahayana Buddhism in the light of quantum physics, it carries no suggestion that the two are complementary or interchangeable. They are, at best, two entirely different orders of looking at "reality," each reflecting completely different underlying processes. That these underlying processes happen to converge at some point is the source of a new paradigm. In his pioneering book *The Tao of Physics*, Fritjof Capra has observed:

> The conception of physical things and phenomena as transient manifestations of an underlying fundamental entity is not only a basic element of quantum field theory, but also a basic element of the Eastern world view... The intuition behind the physicist's interpretation of the subatomic world, in terms of the quantum field, is closely paralleled by that of the Eastern mystic who interprets his

or her experience of the world in terms of an ultimately underlying reality.

Buddhists express the same idea when they call the ultimate reality *shunyata*—"Emptiness" or "the void"—and affirm that it is a living Void which gives birth to all forms in the phenomenal world... Thus the Void of the Eastern mystic can easily be compared to the quantum field of subatomic physics. Like the quantum field, it gives birth to an infinite variety of forms which it sustains and, eventually, reabsorbs.[2]

The effort in this commentary is to see this convergence in a creative light, knowing full well that after convergence the two understandings of reality separate again and their underlying processes take a different turn.

Above all, this commentary on the Heart Sutra is offered in the spirit of a Zen practitioner. It is not intended to be a definitive statement about Mahayana philosophy to be dissected by academic philosophers. This commentary arose out of my own need, and presumably the need of like-minded Zen students, to understand the historical and doctrinal background of this seminal document. But I did not want to get caught in the minutiae of academic analysis and turn this commentary into yet another doctrinal point of view. My focus is not on doctrinal orthodoxy but rather on a radically new understanding of an ancient teaching: the model of the universe set forth in quantum physics.

Since the teaching of the Heart Sutra is centered on insight into "emptiness," the Sanskrit word shunyata (Pali: suññata) is used here throughout, rather than its quite inadequate English translation. It is thus hoped that the inherent vibrancy of shunyata teachings, which have infused the spirit of Mahayana for the last two thousand years, will emerge in the following commentary. Since the developed tradition of Zen bears the imprint of shunyata throughout, it is hoped as well that readers will approach this commentary through the prism of their own meditation practice, and that the vibrancy of their practice will find resonance in the insights of the sutra. As the pioneering scholar

Edward Conze has remarked, "It cannot be the purpose of a commentary to convey directly to the reader the spiritual experiences which a sutra describes. They only reveal themselves to persistent meditation. A commentary must be content to explain the words used."[3]

A note on the English translation of the sutra: There are many translations of the Maha Prajna Paramita Hridaya Sutra (Heart Sutra) now being used by various Zen communities in the United States and Europe. The translation used here is claimed to be based on Kumarajiva's Chinese translation from the early fifth century. It is used by the Kwan Um school of Zen, where I did my own formal Zen training. I am most at home in chanting this version. Other English translations from the same Kumarajiva original may have different renderings. There are difficulties in certain words translated into English from Chinese or Sanskrit. A generation or two of Zen practitioners in the West have become used to chanting their own particular English version, and it's quite hard to change these habits. I hope that these chanting habits can be momentarily set aside to investigate the spirit of the sutra through its textuality.

The Text Itself

The Maha Prajna Paramita Hridaya Sutra

Avalokiteshvara Bodhisattva, when practicing deeply Prajna Paramita, perceives that all five skandhas are empty and is saved from all suffering and distress.

Shariputra, form does not differ from emptiness; emptiness does not differ from form. That which is form is emptiness, that which is emptiness is form. The same is true of feelings, perceptions, impulses, consciousness.

Shariputra, all dharmas are marked with emptiness. They do not appear or disappear, are not tainted or pure, do not increase or decrease. Therefore, in emptiness no form, no feelings, perceptions, impulses, consciousness. No eyes, no ears, no nose, no tongue, no body, no mind, no color, no sound, no smell, no taste, no touch, no object of mind, no realm of eyes, and so forth until no realm of mind consciousness. No ignorance and also no extinction of it, and so forth until no old age and death and also no extinction of them. No suffering, no origination, no stopping, no path, no cognition, also no attainment with nothing to attain.

The bodhisattva depends on Prajna Paramita, and the mind is no hindrance; without any hindrance, no fears exist. Far apart from every perverted view, one dwells in Nirvana.

In the three worlds all buddhas depend on Prajna Paramita and attain Anuttara Samyak Sambodhi.

Therefore know that Prajna Paramita is the great transcendent mantra, is the great bright mantra, is the utmost mantra, is the supreme mantra which is able to relieve all suffering and is true, not false. So proclaim the Prajna Paramita mantra, proclaim the mantra which says:

Gate, gate, paragate, parasamgate, bodhi svaha!

Gate, gate, paragate, parasamgate, bodhi svaha!

Gate, gate, paragate, parasamgate, bodhi svaha!

Background and Setting
of the Sutra

Historical Background of the Sutra

The term "Buddhism," used generically and rather loosely in contemporary Western discourses, is best understood as an ever-evolving phenomenon with three distinct aspects to its history.

First, the *original teachings* of a historical person. This person was, of course, Siddhartha Gautama, who became the Buddha, the Awakened One. These core teachings are the four noble truths, which include the eightfold path, and the chain of dependent origination. There is a historical consensus on the authenticity of these teachings and the teacher. There is also broad agreement among scholars that the discourses contained in the Nikayas (discourse collections) of the Pali canon are the teachings of the historical Buddha.

Second, the Buddhist *philosophy*. This comprises the developed doctrines such as the Abhidhamma canon of the Theravada, the Sarvastivadin, and other orthodox traditions as well as the *sutras* (sermons attributed to the Buddha) and the *shastras* (commentaries on the *sutras*) of the Mahayana tradition, whose composition and compilation took place over a period of centuries after the death of the Buddha. (The Abhidhamma is a compendium of lists and categories for various functions and operations of the human mind that were taught by the Buddha but were not systematized. At the time of the third Buddhist council in ancient India [ca. 250 BCE], a defining moment in Buddhist history, various schools had their own specialized Abhidhamma, most likely for the purposes of monks being able to memorize these categories as part of their monastic learning. Today, only the Abhidhamma of the Theravada remains extant in its original form. However, in early medieval India, it was the Abhidhamma of the Sarvastivadin school that was most influential. The Sanskritized rescension of the subschools of Mahayana is known as Abhidharma.)

Third, the Buddhist *religion*, a smorgasbord of bewildering and seemingly contradictory practices and beliefs ranging from the marathon monks of Mt. Hiei in Japan to the devotees of Pure Land and Nichiren sects in East Asia to lay supporters of forest monks in Thailand and Sri Lanka. The differences among these varieties are more properly the domain of anthropology and sociology.

With regard to these three aspects, it is important to keep in mind that Buddhist thought and practice is a pluralistic tradition in Asia. Buddhism is not a unitary phenomenon. The term "Buddhism" is a nineteenth-century invention, no longer useful or helpful in our twenty-first-century discourses.

"Buddhism" as a unitary designation, bequeathed to us by Christian missionaries of the nineteenth and early twentieth centuries, survives today in the Western mind's compulsive tendency to think in unitary terms. For a trained historian of religions it is important to separate philosophical issues from folk narratives. When done properly, the separation can require a certain quarantining of the philosophical from the folk narratives. This is true as much of Buddhism as it is of Christianity and other religions.

A primary shortcoming in the folk narratives of Buddhism in Asia (and, arguably, in each religious tradition) is that they are essentially local. These local expressions are not always capable of producing a grand narrative, which is often the domain of philosophical and doctrinal traditions. This is a problem that Western expressions of "Buddhism" must contend with. The critical question becomes: What do you do when local folk narratives, inherited from Asian traditions, collide with doctrinal traditions established by scholars in these same Asian Buddhist traditions? One possible strategy is to establish as wide and reliable a context as possible for negotiating the treacherous ground between these two uneasily coexisting facets of the same tradition.

Thus, a reading of the Heart Sutra by a Western practitioner has to balance its central teaching of "emptiness" with its popular and iconic status in the folk narratives of China, Japan, and Korea over the last several centuries. It is helpful to remember that Buddhism flourished in Asia for *millennia* as a folk religion and as an inspiration for civic institutions, both of which are aspects of Buddhist religion. The translation of these frameworks in the modern West, practically and culturally, remains perhaps the most tangled of knots. In many ways these two aspects are the heart and blood of cultural Buddhism, but in some respects they have little or nothing to do with the original teachings.

It should also be noted that many of the texts that would normally be considered part of Buddhist philosophy assign primacy to practices and rituals that may have little to do with Buddha's teachings. A reader or practitioner not born into a Buddhist culture needs to track these boundary crossings in order to create a proper framework for understanding what's being addressed.

Historically, the Heart Sutra, or the Prajna Paramita Hridaya Sutra, to give it its proper Sanskrit name, freely crosses the boundary between Buddhist philosophy and Buddhist religion. The present commentary tries to keep track of such boundary crossings whenever necessary or helpful. The Heart Sutra is arguably the best known of the Mahayana sutras. Chanted daily in Buddhist monasteries in China, Japan, Korea, Tibet, and the West, this short sutra (containing about fourteen verses in Sanskrit and 270 characters in Chinese) is a basic text of Zen tradition and is considered to contain the essence of all Mahayana wisdom schools.

Zen (or Chan) began in China as a meditation school and was shaped mostly by its sutra literature (despite Zen's professed anti-intellectualism). These sutras, originating in ancient India around 200 BCE, capture the dramatic fervor and religious aspirations of new movements that had broken away from the earlier forms of Buddhism. The records of the Third Council (ca. 250 BCE) give us glimpses into various doctrinal experiments carried on by these new schools and movements. This council was convened by King Ashoka (r. ca. 272–236 BCE), who became a great patron of Buddhist communities in ancient India, for the purposes of ascertaining which of the many doctrines then prevalent were in accordance with the teachings of the Buddha. It was at this council that the Abhidhamma (in its Pali rescension) was accepted as the third "basket" (*pitaka*) of Buddha's teachings, the other two being the *sutta-pitaka* ("basket of discourses"), and the *vinaya-pitaka* ("basket of monastic rules of conduct").

Although the term "Mahayana" is of a much later vintage within Indian Buddhism (it is not to be found in the arguments at the Third Council), its doctrines are centered around the teaching of shunyata and the bodhisattva ideal. This ideal exhorts a practitioner to work for the liberation of all beings, however many, rather than striving just for one's own liberation. This ideal developed in contrast to the model of the arahat, the Buddhist saint, of the earlier orthodox tradition, and the new ideal was claimed to be superior in its aspirations. These are the twin teachings of the Prajna Paramita group of sutras of which the Heart Sutra is the core expression. D. T. Suzuki, the great facilitator between the Zen tradition and the West, finds in the psychology of the bodhisattva "one of the greatest achievements of the life of spirit."

The Prajna Paramita sutras, or the sutras of Transcendent Wisdom, are inspirational sources for a number of early rebel or reformist groups that were present at the time of the Third Council. The earliest portions of these sutras go back to the period between 200 BCE and 100 CE; the Heart Sutra itself has been dated by Edward Conze at 350 CE. Another pioneering scholar, Heinrich Dumoulin, tells us:

> The great Mahayana sutras form the center of Mahayana; in them the new religious inspiration is crystallized. A massive and imposing body of literature, the sutras differs greatly in content, but each and every one of them breathes the spirit of Mahayana. These widely scattered writings serve many religious communities. While individual sutras or groups of sutras take up particular themes, they concur and overlap at many points. Moreover, one and the same sutra can give rise to different religious movements. They are often accompanied by explanatory commentaries, or sastras.[4]

When the teachings of the Buddha first moved from India to China in its Mahayana forms, they were known not as Buddhism but as the Religion of Prajna Paramita or, since the sutras of Prajna Paramita centered on the teachings of shunyata, as the Religion of Nothingness. In this chronological framework, the teachings contained in the Prajna Paramita sutras are what might be called proto-Mahayana.

The Heart Sutra is one of approximately thirty-eight sutras in the Prajna Paramita group, and it is the shortest of them. In it the dynamic vibrancy of shunyata and the seemingly cryptic delineation of its meaning have been captured with a radical economy of expression that has fascinated countless generations of Buddhist thinkers in India, China, Tibet, and other lands.

The Heart Sutra scholarship was thrown into disarray in recent years when Jan Nattier wrote a groundbreaking monograph, "The Heart Sutra: A Chinese Apocryphal Text?"[5] in which she argued, on philological evidence, that the present version of the sutra was originally written in Chinese most likely by Kumarajiva in early fifth century CE and excerpted from the larger Prajna Paramita Sutra, re-translated into Sanskrit, and backdated to an Indian origin. If the Nattier thesis is correct, it would detract from the holiness that medieval Chinese Buddhists attributed to texts originating in India. These scholarly wrinkles do not necessarily diminish the historical prominence or popularity of the sutra in Chinese Buddhism (and now in the West), but they call for a new understanding of the sutra, in which it is seen as a Chinese rather than an Indian text.

The popularity and veneration of this sutra in China owes a good deal to the life and adventures of the great pilgrim Xuanzang (Hsuan-tsang; ca. 600–666), who journeyed to India to find the sources of the Buddhism that prevailed in China during his youth. The adversity he had to overcome in his journeys is the stuff of legends and has since become a staple of Chinese popular literature. He reported that during the extremely dangerous crossing of the Taklamakan desert in Central Asia, en route to India, he chanted the Heart Sutra almost nonstop to ward off dangers and difficulties, seen and unseen.

Xuanzang's journey to and stay in India from 628 to 644 CE is one of the great landmarks of Chinese Buddhist history, and is the subject of the popular sixteenth-century Ming romance *Journey to the West*. This epic is to popular Chinese imagination what *Don Quixote* or *Pilgrim's Progress* is to Western literature. Xuanzang's chanting of the Heart Sutra as a *dharani* (magical spell) of immense supernatural power has assumed mythic proportion in the popular Chinese imagination, at times without any reference to the deep insights of the sutra itself. The popularization of the Heart Sutra has been taken to extreme commercial ends in recent years in China, Japan, and Korea through its printing on such items as teacups, hand towels, and neckties.

Xuanzang's deep familiarity with the Heart Sutra suggests that the Kumarajiva translation, done more than two hundred years before Xuanzang's time, had become deeply embedded in Chinese Buddhism, at least within its monastic communities. Xuanzang himself did a highly acclaimed translation of the sutra in 649 upon his return from India. Both he and Kumarajiva are considered to be among the greatest translators of Indian Buddhist texts into Chinese.

Since Xuanzang's time some of the greatest thinkers in Buddhist history—among them Atisa, Fazang (Fa-tsang), Kukai, and Hakuin—have written commentaries on the Heart Sutra. This distinguished commentarial tradition highlights the need of Buddhist practitioners in each generation to understand how this seminal text speaks to them. It is not without interest to note how each generation of practitioners has applied not only its own particular understanding of Buddhist teachings but its cultural prejudices as well to the terminology of the sutra. The perspectives and concerns of the practitioners' milieus are quite distinct in these commentaries. The present commentary's forays into quantum physics and neuroscience are equally indicative of our contemporary culture's concern with its particular frames of reference.

This means that while the Heart Sutra celebrates shunyata as a timeless truth, it must also be seen as a historical document engaged in rivalry with the rationalist-schematic approach taken by the Abhidhamma monks of the orthodox Sarvastivadin school whose doctrines were quite influential in early medieval India. It should also be noted that there were scholarly monks of Mahayana persuasion in early medieval India with their own Abhidharma corpus. Their literature differs in significant details from that of the orthodox schools. In later centuries, while the Abhidhamma remained frozen as a sacred, inviolable text in the countries of Southeast Asia, the Mahayana followers created their own sutra literature to develop and support new indigenous practices and rituals in East Asia.

In the centuries after the Buddha's death, the orthodox Abhidhamma/Abhidharma monks, with their encyclopedic literature, created categories of analysis to the point where it became, in the words of the Zen historian Heinrich Dumoulin, "a dishearteningly lifeless product without metaphysical élan."[6] Mahayana sutras thunder again and again against philosophers (Abhidharmists) who are disposed to freeze reality into a categorical permanence and to discriminate between subject and object.

Doctrinally, the Heart Sutra seems to be a specific rejoinder to the Abhidhamma schema of the Sarvastivadin school that had become dominant in Indian Buddhism after the downfall of the Maurya dynasty (ca. second century BCE). Various responses to Sarvastivadin doctrines lie at the genesis of the movement that later came to be called Mahayana, and the Heart Sutra is a crucial text in the evolution of that movement.

Briefly stated, the Sarvastivadin Abhidhamma advocated a radical theory of pluralism that sought to affirm the existence of momentary entities (*dharmas*) in the past, present, and future simultaneously. Their important contribution to the theory of time need not detain us; their central argument was that reality is a complex system of dharmas. These building blocks of the universe cannot be reduced further—they are thus "ultimates"—but they can be known; and liberation consists of such knowledge. The Sarvastivadins offered a list of seventy-five dharmas, which, like the theory of *atoms* in Greek philosophy, represent final, indivisible units. In the Sarvastivadin view these dharmas are real; they have existed from beginningless time and only change from a latent to a manifest state. These Sarvastivadin doctrines were trigger points that invited a response from Mahayana monks whose orientation was already shifting toward practices of faith and devotion. They were making a fundamental shift from analytical knowledge (of the dharmas) to gnosis (intuitive or mystical knowledge).

Why this prominence of the orthodox Sarvastivadin school in the scheme of things? Largely it's a matter of history and geography. After being excluded from the patronage network in the aftermath of the Third Council, the monks of the Sarvastivadin school moved from the eastern (Magadhan) to the northwestern part of India (present-day Kashmir). This was also the region where other nascent Mahayana forms of practice and philosophy developed. By the time of Nagarjuna (ca. second century CE) the northwestern part of India was the new and vital center of Buddhist practice and doctrinal development.

Nagarjuna is the most important of Mahayana thinkers; he is indeed the foundational teacher of all Mahayana philosophy. His dialectic of Madhyamika (Middle Way) has formed the basis of all subsequent Mahayana philosophy. In a roundabout way the Heart Sutra is a cogent and concise summation of what Nagarjuna conveys in his extremely sophisticated dialectic. The key difference is that the Heart Sutra was most likely written for purposes of memorization by monks and laypeople alike and also as a shortcut to reinforcing core Mahayana teachings of shunyata and the bodhisattva's path.

In the still-solidifying tradition of Mahayana, the Heart Sutra is a key document that demolishes all categories of plurality and dualism and points out that such categorical thinking is not conducive for the cultivation of wisdom that leads to awakening. In the earliest stages of the formation of Mahayana, some schools of thought proposed a doctrine of "five words" of the Buddha. According to this doctrine, meditation on these words alone has transcendental significance and the power to bring liberation (which, they claimed, was not the case with the rest of the discourses). These five words are: non-self (Pali: *anatta*, Skt: *anatman*); impermanence (*anicca*, *anitya*); anguish or stress (*dukkha*); transcendence (*nibbana, nirvana*); and emptiness (*suññata, shunyata*).

The school most prominently associated with the doctrine of five words as transcendental was the school of Bahushrutiyas ("those who have heard many teachings"). This school was itself a subschool of Lokottaravada, a school whose main argument was that the Buddha was a transcendental (*lokottara*) "principle" rather than a historical person. According to its followers the teachings of this transcendental principle can be divided into the mundane (for worldly understanding) and the transcendental (for final liberation). The position espoused by the followers of the Lokottaravada and Bahushrutiyas led to a transhistorical understanding of the Buddha and, in due course, opened the door to a fascination with the mystical and the magical, especially in Chinese and other East Asian cultures. Many practices in folk Buddhist traditions are, understandably, a continuation of this fascination. A fascination with the magico-mantic is equally prevalent in the Buddhist countries of Southeast Asia, where Abhidhamma is the main textual source. The most prominent of such instances is the Buddhism of Burma (now Myanmar), where the scholastic and the folkloric coexist somewhat uneasily.

Early Mahayanists share the first four of the "five words" with the Nikaya tradition of Pali Buddhism; it is with the inclusion of the fifth word, shunyata, that early Mahayana asserts its differences with the orthodox schools. Thus it may be argued that shunyata is the only real doctrinal innovation of early Indian Mahayana philosophy. But then again, the term is not entirely absent in the Pali discourses. For the Nikaya followers, the term *shunyata*—emptiness—may have been synonymous with *anatta*—non-self or no-soul—but the latter term had restricted use in describing persons. The Mahayana invention was to postulate shunyata as the essential emptiness of the phenomenal world, including the world within a person's mind.

The thinkers of Mahayana schools took care to deny the existence of shunyata as yet another category. Consequently, we have the teaching of *shunyata-shunyatam* (emptiness of emptiness) in the later tradition, which warns against the dangers of conceptualizing shunyata as a thing-in-itself. Shunyata is an insight or wisdom that's captured in wordless intuition. In Mahayana understanding, it is only through this intuitive wisdom that one can realize the true nature of the phenomenal world, let go of all clinging to it, and reach the "other shore" of liberation.

The popularity of the Heart Sutra in Buddhist tradition lies not only in its brevity but also in the elusiveness of its meaning. Distinguished commentators over the ages have formulated a wide diversity of interpretations of it, which has led Edward Conze to observe that the [commentators] "tell us more what the text meant to them within their own culture than what the Indian original intended to convey."[7]

Thus Kukai (the founder of Shingon Buddhism) in ninth-century Japan speaks on the Heart Sutra from a tantric point of view that is practically impossible to understand for someone who has not been initiated into its esoteric ritual intricacies. But it nonetheless shows Kukai's distinctive interpretation of classical Indian Mahayana doctrines.

Similarly, in the Indo-Tibetan tradition, Kamalashila in eighth-century Tibet stakes out a position that is still central to the Tibetan understanding of the Heart Sutra, most notably in Kamalashila's influence on the seminal Tibetan master Tsongkhapa several centuries later. Today Tsongkhapa (1357–1419) is to Tibetan Buddhist tradition what St. Thomas Aquinas is to medieval Christianity—the font of all inviolable doctrinal frameworks.

The commentary on the Heart Sutra by Hakuin Ekaku, the Rinzai Zen master who revitalized koan study in Japan in the eighteenth-century is quite unlike any "spiritual" text one is likely to come across. If it were not for the fact that Hakuin was one of the greatest Zen masters in history, it would be easy enough to suspect his interpretation as inspired more by the pharmaceutical than the doctrinal. How else is one to understand Hakuin's description of the famous line "Form is no other than emptiness; emptiness no other than form," as "A lame turtle with painted eyebrows stands in the evening breeze"?[8]

All this goes to show that perhaps all the divergent interpretations of the Heart Sutra are somehow appropriate, each in its own way, since the elusive meaning of shunyata demands that each generation of Buddhist thinkers and practitioners in each culture come to grips with it through the praxis of experience.

The Heart Sutra has two versions, the longer and the shorter. The longer version, available to us in the Indo-Tibetan tradition, has a prologue in which the Buddha enters into *samadhi* (concentration) and an epilogue in which he rises from samadhi and praises the bodhisattva Avalokiteshvara, who had just spoken what has become the text of the shorter Heart Sutra. The shorter version, available principally through the Zen tradition and discussed here, begins without the prologue and has Avalokiteshvara contemplating the meaning of the profound perfection of wisdom. This shorter version also has no epilogue.

The Setting

In traditional telling, the Heart Sutra was preached on Vulture Peak, east of the ancient Indian city of Rajagriha, the capital of the kingdom of Magadha. Rajagriha was one of the two major cities of ancient India most frequently visited by the Buddha during his forty-five years of teaching. Vulture Peak is said to have been a favorite site of his, and here he gave a number of sermons to assemblies of monks and laypeople. Many of the texts recorded in the Pali canon of early Buddhism were spoken at Vulture Peak.

The prologue in the longer version of the sutra introduces us to the leading characters: Shakyamuni Buddha, Avalokiteshvara Bodhisattva, and Shariputra, one of the chief disciples of the Buddha renowned for insights into *anatta* or not-self. The Buddha does not speak in the prologue but enters into samadhi and silently empowers Shariputra to ask and Avalokiteshvara to answer. The silence of the Buddha here is characteristic of much of Mahayana literature, and supports its classical view that the Buddha is "no longer simply the teacher but is transformed into the principle of enlightenment, a silent, eternal, numinous presence, the *dharmakaya* [the self-identification of an awakened mind with everything else in the universe]."⁹

The Heart Sutra is the only Prajna Paramita text in which the bodhisattva Avalokiteshvara appears. Avalokiteshvara's presence here is significant on several counts: first, it attests to the relatively late date of the sutra, a time when the cult of the bodhisattva of compassion had become well established. Avalokiteshvara is this bodhisattva's name in Indian Mahayana; in Chinese it is Kuan Yin or Guanyin; in Japanese, Kannon or Kanzeon; in Korean, Kwan Se Um. The first significant mention of this bodhisattva of compassion is to be found in the twenty-fourth chapter of the Lotus Sutra which also became a basis for Pure Land sutras in later generations. *Ava* means "looking down" or "beholding"; *loka* is the phenomenal world, and *lokita* refers to its doings; and *ishvara* means, literally, the lord or the deity. So the name

Avalokiteshvara literally means "the lord who looks down at the world from above."

In another related etymological formation, the root verb for *ishvara* is *svara*, or "sound." This would lead to a parallel translation as "the lord who hears the sounds or cries of the world." Thus, a full understanding of "Avalokiteshvara" as it has emerged in the folk narratives of East Asia is "the lord who beholds the doings of the phenomenal world and hears its cries with compassion."

In iconographical representations, this bodhisattva has a thousand arms and an eye in the palm of each hand, through which she is able to help all those who seek her help in ways that are skillfully appropriate to each person's need. These iconographical representations also show worldly beings floundering in the sea of samsara while the bodhisattva looks down from above.

The bodhisattva of compassion transformed from a male figure in Indian Buddhism to a female figure in China, Japan, Korea, and Tibet; this transformation remains one of the great mysteries of the Mahayana Buddhism that developed in North and East Asia. In traditional patriarchal societies, male archetypes were associated with the roles of priest, warrior, and merchant; and religious and social hierarchies arose from these roles. These same societies associated compassion and caring with feminine qualities and assigned them to female deities in the religious pantheon. It is likely that as Buddhism evolved in early medieval China, the Taoist model of harmonizing the two polar energies of *yin* and *yang* (yin as the feminine, compassionate, soft, nurturing, yielding, receptive; yang as the masculine, energetic, proactive, hard, unyielding) may have played a pivotal role in providing a complementary background for the Mahayana's balance of wisdom and compassion.

Why was this balance needed? The early Mahayana practitioners in India may have felt that the extraordinary emphasis on wisdom in the earlier Pali Nikaya tradition caused or could cause one-sidedness in the understanding of the Buddha's teachings. Although compassion is present in the Pali Nikayas as a quality to be cultivated, its role in these texts is secondary to the cultivation of wisdom. The innovation in Mahayana Buddhism was to raise compassion to equal standing, to somehow balance the shocking intensity of the wisdom of emptiness with a leavening of healing and helping through compassion.

The care and love given by a mother to a child is easy to associate with the bodhisattva of compassion as a female archetype. What seems to emerge from the narratives of folk Buddhism throughout China, Japan, and Korea is the quality of care the supplicant expects to find in seeking a refuge in the bodhisattva of compassion.[10]

"Compassion" is primarily a linguistic and doctrinal subject in Indian Prajna Paramita sutras, whereas the bodhisattva of compassion in East Asian representations is an iconographical embodiment of the same subject. Iconography moves us into the realm of the believer-practitioner, the folkloric, and the anthropological.

That the Heart Sutra is a text for the practitioner-believer implies that its meaning and understanding are no longer an exclusive province of the Indian Mahayana philosopher but have become the heritage of the Chinese, Japanese, or Korean practitioner.

On the face of it, the Heart Sutra is completely dedicated to the teaching of shunyata without any reference whatever to compassion, which traditionally includes the *upaya*, or "skillful means," of the bodhisattva. The absence of the theme of compassion in the Heart Sutra is countered, implicitly, by the fact that the wisdom essential for the attainment of buddhahood is proclaimed by a bodhisattva who is the very embodiment of compassion.

The presence of Shariputra is equally significant. The Heart Sutra does not inveigh against the *shravakas* (disciples of the Buddha, literally "hearers"), as is characteristic of the longer Mahayana sutras where *shravakas* are considered inferior to the bodhisattvas both in wisdom and in aspiration to enlightenment. The presence of Shariputra in the Heart Sutra provides the polemical foil. In Pali scriptures Shariputra is considered the wisest of the disciples of the Buddha. His historical role as the founder of the Abhidhamma scholastic approach is decisive within Pali Buddhism. Here he is presented as being perplexed and unable to understand the deeper meaning of shunyata teaching. The "wisdom" with which Shariputra is associated is an understanding of the categorical analyses of Abhidhamma, whose chief assertion is the view that dharmas are ultimate units of experience. The assertion here is that the highest form of wisdom—*Prajna Paramita*—is that all units of experience are ultimately empty, and that the teaching of shunyata begins where Abhidhamma ends. The sutra thus deconstructs the previous Abhidhamma understanding of dharmas and articulates a new framework for how the dharmas should be understood.

Commentary

The Title: *Maha Prajna Paramita Hridaya Sutra*

Maha means great or large. *Prajna* means wisdom, and more specifically, intuitive, preverbal wisdom. *Paramita* is commonly translated as "perfection," although in a different etymological usage it can also mean "that which has gone beyond" or "transcendental." *Hridaya* means "heart," but, as mentioned earlier, its context here is that of heart-mind. The word *hridaya* may also be understood as a "core" or "essence" rather than a physical organ. *Sutra* is the spoken word, which, in the Buddhist tradition, is the sermon or words spoken by the Buddha. Thus the full meaning of the title can be either "The Great Heart of Perfect Wisdom" or "The Heart of Great Transcendent Wisdom." Or we may use poetic license to translate it as "The Wisdom of the Great Heart of the Universe"—this would certainly be in keeping with the insight that the sutra offers into shunyata as the core of the universe.

Avalokiteshvara Bodhisattva...

Avalokiteshvara is a celestial bodhisattva in Mahayana cosmology and is an embodiment of compassion. A recent work of significant scholarship offers cultural and social insights into this gender transformation from a male figure in Indian tradition to a female figure in Chinese tradition.[11]

The imagery most often associated with Guanyin, the Chinese form, is that of a bodhisattva who hears and beholds the cries and struggles of beings drowning in the ocean of samsara, and reaches down to pull them up. The Tibetan name for Avalokiteshvara is Chenrezig, meaning one "who always has his eyes open," who is always compassionately aware of the suffering of all beings.

The word *bodhisattva* is a composite of *bodhi*, which means being awake or enlightened, and *sattva*, meaning a living being. In Mahayana understanding, bodhisattvas are beings who have diligently cultivated the qualities necessary for becoming a buddha. We have seen above that the determining factor for their actions is a boundless compassion informed by the supreme wisdom of shunyata. These compassionate acts are skillful, but they are not personalized. This means that the compassion of the bodhisattva is directed not to the suffering person's personal narrative but to the person's general condition of being caught in the net of karmic transgressions. Although this is not the place to go into a lengthy discussion of the issue, this paradigm of the bodhisattva as a helping being is essentially different from that of a psychotherapist whose engagement is with the personal narrative of the client. The bodhisattva's engagement acknowledges the personal narrative but focuses on the much larger vision of existence, suffering, karma, and rebirth.

The Mahayana distinguishes two kinds of bodhisattvas—earthly and transcendental. Earthly bodhisattvas live a life of compassion and service to others as an expression of their commitment to working toward liberation. Transcendental bodhisattvas are sometimes called bodhisattva-mahasattva. They are those who have actualized all the paramitas (perfections) and have attained buddhahood, but they have postponed their entry into complete, remainderless nirvana. They are in possession of perfect wisdom and are no longer subject to the workings of samsara. They are also in possession of all *upaya-paramita* or the perfection of skillful means necessary to help beings caught up in samsara. In popular imagination, they can manifest themselves to believers in earthly forms.

Just as Avalokiteshvara is a representation of compassion in Mahayana Buddhism, so the bodhisattva Manjushri is an embodiment of wisdom. Both are transcendental bodhisattvas and they balance and reinforce each other. Together they represent the core qualities of a bodhisattva in Mahayana formulations. The implication is that a buddha, as the perfected bodhisattva, whether the historical Shakyamuni or a transhistorical figure, is the embodiment of a perfect balance of wisdom and compassion.

…when practicing deeply Prajna Paramita…

In the prologue of the longer version of the sutra, this line depicts the Buddha as being immersed in deep samadhi while the bodhisattva Avalokiteshvara too is absorbed in contemplating the meaning of the perfection of wisdom. The statement is significant here in that the tradition insists that "a looking into" the nature of reality is not a matter of mere intellectual analysis (which the followers of Mahayana accused the Abhidharmist monks of doing) but demands deep absorption, so that awareness moves from the merely superficial to the profoundly intuitive. This is true for the celestial bodhisattva as it is for each earthly practitioner. Other translations of "practicing deeply" are "deep realization" or "dwelling in the depths of Prajna Paramita." The idea here is the cultivation of the deep wisdom necessary for seeing directly into the nature of things.

In Mahayana cosmology, Prajna Paramita (perfection of wisdom) is seen as the "mother of all buddhas." If we interpret the mother as a source from which all things are born, we will understand the wisdom of shunyata or emptiness as the source of liberation for all buddhas and bodhisattvas. All bodhisattvas, whether earthly or celestial, meditate continually on the wisdom of shunyata.

...perceives that all five skandhas are empty...

In this deep contemplation of the wisdom of shunyata the bodhisattva perceives the five *skandhas* to be empty. The word *perceives* here is synonymous with having *insight into* or having *deep realization of* [emptiness of all phenomena]. It is an insight, a realization of deep truth that throws light on what was previously misunderstood. It is an act of purification of ignorance. In the deepest meaning of the term, it is not an actual person who perceives or has realization, but rather a purified awareness itself that witnesses deep truth. Or, to put it another way, it is not some technical knowledge that belongs to a person's resumé but an ongoing process of seeing deeply into the nature of things. The function of this insight is to reconfigure one's own ways of being in the world so that the conditioned existence is now tuned to the wholesome and helpful to oneself and others.

Next, before we look at the term *skandha*, it might be useful to deal first with some of the complexities around the term "emptiness," since it is the central teaching not only of the Heart Sutra but also of the entire Mahayana literature. A translation of the Sanskrit word *shunyata* into Western languages has always been problematic. When translated as "void" or "emptiness" it has a nihilistic undertone, which is how the Orientalists of the nineteenth century understood and portrayed Buddhism. Fortunately our understanding of the term—and of Buddhist teachings—has grown in recent decades and has prevailed over earlier misinterpretations.

The word *shunyata* is composed of *shunya* (empty) + *ta* (belonging to). The root of the word *shunya* itself comes from the verb *svi*, meaning "to swell up." At the same time, the term *shunya* (Pali: *suñña*) means, among other things, an uninhabited place. Thus, from the very beginning, the root verb sets up a difficulty of understanding what has swelled up and what is empty. The metaphors used to illuminate this dilemma in the compound term *shunyata* are a swelling or a bubble or an uninhabited hut. In each case there appears to be an identifiable form that encloses something. What is seen are enclosures; and our commonsense view is that enclosures must contain something. The reality, however, is that each enclosure in these metaphors is hollow or contentless. Today's physics probably has mathematical formulations that will show how a swelling or a bubble comes into manifestation without there being any content.

In the Buddhist wisdom tradition, the compound term *shunyata* serves the function of distinguishing between appearance and reality. When one is deluded, one assumes that what is apprehended by the senses (that is, the bubble) contains something identifiable or graspable; the corrective application of *prajna* (wisdom, or in this context insight into shunyata) allows one to see that all appearances are made up of different components and are therefore illusory, not real in themselves, and that there is nothing inherent in them that can be grasped, appropriated, or owned. Grasping an illusion will only lead to delusion. Prajna does not automatically invalidate appearances, but rather challenges us to investigate the issue of "essence" more closely.

Shunyata is a concept that appears in the Pali canon but was generally ignored by the Abhidhamma systematizers. In the Pali suttas, this term was used in a double sense. First, it referred to a direct mode of perception in which nothing is added to or subtracted from the data perceived. This modality of perception perceives thought as a thought, irrespective of its contents, without attending to the question of whether or not there is a thinker. When an object is apprehended in the visual field, there is simply the experience of seeing without either an affirmation or denial of the object's existence. And this is true for auditory or other sense objects.

In recent years, a technique closely following this methodology has been perfected by an outstanding Burmese teacher of vipassana meditation, Mahasi Sayadaw (1904–1982), called "noting" practice or "bare attention." In this modality nirvana is considered to be the highest form of shunyata of the phenomenal world, in the sense of, first, an uncorrupted mode of awareness of things as they are, and, second, a lack of a selfhood (anything capable of autonomous sustainment) in the six senses and their objects. In other words, shunyata is both a mode of perception and an attribute of things perceived.[12]

The Mahayana articulation of shunyata is not essentially different from the original understanding in the Pali canon. The problem for early Mahayanists arose when the Abhidharmist philosophers seemed to claim (who said what is a matter of dispute) that even though an individual person was empty of self, there were dharmas that had their "own-being" (*svabhava*) and were the building blocks of the universe. In a certain sense this theory is akin to the Newtonian particle theory in physics. Early Mahayana thinkers attacked this notion and accused the Abhidharmists of being attached to a subtle notion of "self" in the dharmas, of being substantialists, and thus unable to truly understand the Buddha's teachings.

These Mahayana thinkers buttressed their arguments with new developments in linguistics and mathematics at the time. Panini (ca. fourth century BCE), the great founder of Sanskrit grammar, had introduced the concept of zero which became a lynchpin of applying mathematics to linguistics. Pictorially, zero was a round circle with nothing inside. This picture seemed to match the Mahayana thinkers' understanding of the term *shunya*: an enclosure but nothing inside, or the essential contentlessness of the phenomena. In other words, manifestation without essence.

> In the fourth century BCE, the linguist Panini had developed the concept of *zero* (Sanskrit, *shunya*) to symbolize empty but functioning positions in his analysis of Sanskrit grammar. (He proposed that every word was composed of a root and a suffix, so words without suffixes actually had the zero suffix.) Mathematicians eventually borrowed the concept to supply an essential principle of the decimal notation we use today: that a place in a system may be empty (like the zeros in 10,000) but can still function in relationship to the rest of the system.[13]

The central doctrinal controversy between the Abhidharmists and the early Mahayana thinkers thus rested on the former's assertion that the irreducible dharmas forming the ultimate building blocks of experience were each endowed with svabhava, its own particular being or nature. The Mahayanists posited that all dharmas were *empty of* svabhava. Even though conditional relations (between dharmas) functioned as interdependent co-arising,

> there were no "essences" acting as nodes in the relationships, just as mathematical relationships could function among the integers in the decimal notation even if they were only zeroes. In fact, if dharmas had any essence, the principles of causation and the Four Noble Truths could not operate, for essences by nature cannot change, and thus cannot be subject to causal conditions. Whether the Abhidharmists meant the concept of *svabhava* to imply an unchanging essence is a moot point, but in time the doctrine of emptiness became a rallying point for the rejection of the entire Abhidharma enterprise.[14]

It's easier for us these days to understand the controversy between the Abhidharmists and the early Mahayana thinkers through parallel developments in Newtonian atomic theory (corresponding to the Abhidhamma position) and in quantum subatomic theory (corresponding to the Mahayana position). Our current understanding of Buddhist meditative experiences has also been greatly facilitated by the findings of quantum physics with regard to the nature of ultimate reality; these findings have added a new dimension to our efforts to understand the meaning of shunyata.

The Newtonian/Cartesian view of the world has long rested on the notion of solid, indestructible particles as the building blocks of matter and all life—particles moving in space, influencing one another through gravitation, and interacting according to fixed and unchangeable laws. This myth disintegrated under the impact of the experimental and theoretical evidence produced by quantum physicists in the early decades of the twentieth century. The experiments of quantum physics showed that atoms, the presumed fundamental building blocks of the universe, were essentially empty. In experiments subatomic particles showed the same paradoxical nature as light, manifesting either as particles or as waves depending on how the experiment was set up. Quantum physicists, confronting the mysteries of the universe, were left with language that evokes Zen koans: the sound of a quark, the shape of a resonance, the nature of strangeness!

Quantum physics has thus brought about a radical new understanding both of the particles and the void. In subatomic physics mass is no longer seen as a material substance but is recognized as a form of energy

George Leonard, one of the founders of the Human Potential Movement in the 1960s and 1970s, has been a leading figure in understanding the convergence of Eastern wisdom and Western science. His book, *The Silent Pulse*, from which the following passage is adapted, speaks eloquently of energy configurations both in physics and in the human body through such disciplines as Aikido and Tai chi.

[When a piece of seemingly solid matter—a rock, a human hand, the limb of a tree—is placed under a powerful electronic microscope],

the electron-scanning microscope, with the power to magnify several thousand times, takes us down into a realm that has the look of the sea about it. In the kingdom of the corpuscles, there is transfiguration and there is *samsara*, the endless round of birth and death. Every passing second, some 2.5 million red cells are born; every second, the same number die. The typical cell lives about 110 days, then becomes tired and decrepit. There are no lingering deaths here, for when a cell loses its vital force, it somehow attracts the attention of macrophage.

As the magnification increases, the flesh does begin to dissolve. Muscle fiber now takes on a fully crystalline aspect. We can see that it is made of long, spiral molecules in orderly array. And all of these molecules are swaying like wheat in the wind, connected with one another and held in place by invisible waves that pulse many trillions of times a second.

What are the molecules made of? As we move closer, we see atoms, the tiny shadowy balls dancing around their fixed locations in the molecules, sometimes changing position with their partners in perfect rhythms. And now we focus on one of the atoms; its interior is lightly veiled by a cloud of electrons. We come closer, increasing the magnification. The shell dissolves and we look on the inside to find... nothing.

Somewhere within that emptiness, we know is a nucleus. We scan the space, and there it is, a tiny dot. At last, we have discovered something hard and solid, a reference point. But no! As we move closer to the nucleus, it too begins to dissolve. It too is nothing more than an oscillating field, waves of rhythm. Inside the nucleus are other organized fields: protons, neutrons, even smaller "particles." Each of these, upon our approach, also dissolves into pure rhythm.

These days they (the scientists) are looking for quarks, strange subatomic entities, having qualities which they describe with such words as upness, downness, charm, strangeness, truth, beauty, color, and flavor. But no matter. If we could get close enough to these wondrous quarks, they too would melt away. They too would have to give up all pretense of solidity. Even their speed and relationship would be unclear, leaving them only relationship and pattern of vibration.

Of what is the body made? It is made of emptiness and rhythm. At the ultimate heart of the body, at the heart of the world, there is no solidity. Once again, there is only the dance.

[At] the unimaginable heart of the atom, the compact nucleus, we have found no solid object, but rather a dynamic pattern of tightly confined energy vibrating perhaps 1022 times a second: a dance. The protons—the positively charged knots in the pattern of the nucleus—are not only powerful, they are very old. Along with the much lighter electrons that spin and vibrate around the outer regions of the atom, the protons constitute the most ancient entities of matter in the universe, going back to the first seconds after the birth of space and time.[15]

It follows then that in the world of subatomic physics there are no objects, only processes. Atoms consist of particles and these particles are not made of any solid material substance. When we observe them under a microscope, we never see any substance; we observe dynamic patterns, continually changing into one another—a continuous dance of energy. This dance of energy, the underlying rhythm of the universe, is more intuited than seen. Jack Kornfield, a contemporary teacher of meditation, finds a parallel between the behavior of subatomic particles and meditational states:

When the mind becomes very silent, you can clearly see that all that exists in the world are brief moments of consciousness arising together with the six sense objects. There is only sight and the knowing of sight, sound and the knowing of sound, smell, taste and the knowing of them, thoughts and the knowing of thoughts. If you can make the mind very focused, as you can in meditation, you see that the whole breaks down into these small events of sight and the knowing, sound and the knowing and thought and the knowing. No longer are there houses, cars, bodies, or even oneself. All you see are particles of consciousness as experience. Yet you can go deep in meditation in another way and the mind becomes very still. You will see differently that consciousness is like waves, like a sea, an ocean. Now it is not particles but instead every sight and sound is contained in this ocean of consciousness. From this perspective, there is no sense of particles at all.[16]

Energy, whether of wave or particle, is associated with activity, with dynamic change. Thus the core of the universe—whether we see it as the heart of the atom or our own consciousness—is not static but in constant and dynamic change. This energy—now wave, now particle—infuses each and every form at the atomic level. No form exists without being infused by this universal energy; form and energy interpenetrate each other endlessly in an ever-changing dance of molecules, creating our universe. This universal energy is itself a process beyond the confines of time and space. A form, on the other hand, is an event existing momentarily in time and space. This "moment" may last for seventy or eighty years in the case of a human being, a thousand years in the case of a sequoia tree, a few million years in the case of a mountain, but internally, at the subatomic level, each of these forms is in a process of change at any given moment. In the paradigm of quantum physics there is ceaseless change at the core of the universe; in the paradigm of Mahayana wisdom too there is ceaseless change at the core of our consciousness and of the universe.

But change implies alteration from one thing to something else. Without some *thing* to be changed, there would be no instantiation of change. Without forms, there would be no change; without the energy of change, the forms would not be able to hold their balance and would collapse. In meditation practice we see this dynamic, constant change in our own mind-body system.

It has been just as difficult for the human mind to accept shunyata, or empty co-origination at the core of the universe, as it was for the early quantum physicists to accept the quantum randomness of the universe. Einstein had even hoped that the quantum theory he helped create was somehow flawed, wishing desperately, even in the face of the evidence of his own experiments, that there would be a hidden variable that would establish order in the quantum world. Unable to refute the new physics, Einstein spent the rest of his life in a futile search for a unified theory based not on quantum mechanics but relativity. To his contemporaries, his desperation seemed like a search for the "God particle," something seen as daft, even obstructionist.

Later experiments, conducted at the University of California in Berkeley on Bell's theorem [named after the physicist John S. Bell who argued that the experiments of quantum mechanics show that the universe is not locally deterministic, and that the limits of local hidden variables will be exceeded by measurements performed on entangled pairs of particles], confirmed the absence of any hidden variable, and showed that when either of two correlated particles were observed, no matter how far separated in the space, the other was instantly affected by the observation—as if the two particles were embedded in the observing consciousness itself. Even before Bell's theorem, Werner Heisenberg, one of the founding fathers of quantum theory, formulated in his uncertainty principle that it is not possible to examine a situation or system without altering the system. Similarly, in the deepest experience of meditation the object of consciousness is embedded in the observing consciousness; the two are fused together by the energy, or shunyata, out of which both emerge.

A strange place is this world of the new physicists, a world of ultimate connectedness, where consciousness—or observership, as John Wheeler calls it—coexisted with the creation, and where it might be said that the vastness of space, the nuclear conflagration of stars, the explosions of galaxies are simply mechanism for producing that first glimmer of awareness in your baby's eyes.[17]

Subatomic particles, then, are dynamic patterns, processes rather than objects. Shunyata too is a dynamic pattern rather than an entity. Henry Stapp, an atomic physicist, has remarked, "An elementary particle is not an independently existing unanalyzable entity. It is, in essence, a set of relationships that reach outward to other things."[18]

Compare this to Nagarjuna (the great Buddhist thinker, ca. second century CE, who, in his dialectic of Madhyamika, sought to define the core understanding of Mahayana wisdom): "Things derive their being and nature by mutual dependence and are nothing in themselves."[19]

Nagarjuna's formulation of the Middle Way—between being and nonbeing, between existence and nihilism—holds that underneath the absence of all substances, qualities, or essential characteristics of this changing world there still remains an ultimate reality. This ultimate reality is that of dependent origination. Much misunderstanding has taken place in later Mahayana tradition in the contextualization of this "ultimate reality."

For Nagarjuna, this ultimate reality of dependent origination (Pali: *paticca-samuppada*; Skt: *pratitya-samutpada*, an elaboration of the second noble truth of the Buddha) is a process and not a thing-in-itself, and it applies equally to all phenomena. The function of prajna, or seeing directly into the nature of things, is to apprehend this ultimate reality of dependent origination.

For the quantum physicist the ultimate reality may be the interplay of energy between wave and particle, something that can be intuited at the other end of an electron microscope! Neither wave nor particle is a thing-in-itself. Prajna gives us the same insight: there is no thing-in-itself; each thing is an effect of some causal condition.

Thus our understanding of the word *shunyata* becomes a bit clearer. All forms are momentary manifestations in time and space; while the form lasts, it has validity (which is different from "reality"), but this appearance is transitory and illusory if this appearance is seen as a thing-in-itself. Thus a more appropriate and accessible way to understand shunyata may be to understand it as "momentariness" or "transitoriness" rather than emptiness.

The doctrinal innovation in Nagarjuna and Mahayana philosophy is to make a clear distinction between the conventional and the ultimate. From an ultimate point of view, all things are empty of svabhava, that is, all things are really processes, never things-in-themselves. From a conventional point of view, all things are momentary or transitory appearances and are valid as such only momentarily. In their momentary validity, they can be engaged with, but not clung to. This is the central teaching of all buddhas. Such an engagement takes place through prajna and skillful means.

The core teaching of the Buddha always has been that all things are dependently arisen, hence fundamentally devoid of any independently lasting substance. All that's happening in the phenomenal world is an interplay of form and energy that creates a transitory phenomenon in time and space. In our ignorance, we continue to interpret this interplay as real-in-itself. Moreover, as captives of linguistic formulations we even interpret our conceptual thinking to represent something real.

Nagarjuna cautions us against the temptation to posit shunyata as a category and reminds us again and again that shunyata itself is empty (*shunyata-shunyatam*). The only way to apprehend the dynamic nature of shunyata is by means of an intuitive seeing-through of the transitory /momentary nature of forms. If there were no manifestations of form, the principles of shunyata and dependent origination would be an irrelevant issue.

In *The Tao of Physics*, Fritjof Capra makes a similar observation:

> The phenomenal manifestations of the mystical Void, like the subatomic particles, are not static and permanent, but dynamic and transitory, coming into being and vanishing in one ceaseless dance of movement and energy. Like the subatomic world of the physicist, the phenomenal world of the Eastern mystic is a world of *samsara*—of continuous birth and death. Being transient manifestations of the Void, the things in the world do not have any fundamental identity. This is especially emphasized in Buddhist philosophy which denies the existence of any material substance and also holds that the idea of a constant "self" undergoing successive experiences is an illusion.[20]

As we have seen above, in Sanskrit language *shunya* is also the word for zero. In the Western intellectual tradition, a circle or a zero represents nothingness. In Native American usage, a circle means coming together, a sharing. In Chinese philosophical usage, a circle means totality, wholeness. As Garma C. C. Chang, the noted Buddhist scholar, has remarked,

Zero itself contains nothing, yet it cannot be held to be absolutely or nihilistically void. As a mathematical concept and symbol, zero has a great many functions and utilities, without which it would be practically impossible to execute business and scientific activities in this modern age. If someone asked you, "Is zero nothingness?" you would be hard pressed to give an appropriate reply. Zero is both nothing and the possibility of everything. It is definitely not something nihilistically empty, rather it is dynamic and vital to all manifestations. In the same way, *Shunyata* does not mean complete nothingness; being "serenely vibrant," it has both negative and positive facets.[21]

In the same vein Masao Abe, another noted contemporary Buddhist thinker, has remarked that for Nagarjuna emptiness was not nonbeing but "wondrous Being." Moreover, "precisely because it is Emptiness which 'empties' even emptiness, true Emptiness (Absolute Nothingness) is absolute Reality which makes all phenomena, all existents, truly be."[22]

Abe's language of "Absolute Nothingness" is a central feature of the philosophy of the Kyoto School, the pioneering attempt to marry classical Zen understanding with the language of twentieth-century Western, especially German, philosophy. Behind all the technicalities of this language, there lies the simple idea, propounded by the Buddha, of dependent arising as the absolute principle of the phenomenal world. Abe and other thinkers of the Kyoto School take the edge off any nihilistic implications a discussion about shunyata might have. This is in keeping with classical Mahayana philosophy originating in India. This positivistic approach allows Mahayana thinkers to offer compassion (*karuna*) as a counterpoint to wisdom (*shunyata*).

Some Zen teachers articulate shunyata positively as boundlessness. The image often associated with this articulation is that of the great ocean, its vastness, and its seeming lack of confinement. The notion of boundlessness may also find some resonance in an understanding of quantum energy as a sea of churning energy which is not bound by any seeming order, hierarchical system, or prescriptive rules or protocols. Quantum energy organizes its wave-particle equation through the participation of the observer; similarly, insight into boundlessness organizes itself through the nonclinging awareness of the observer.

In quantum theory, there is a higher degree of organizational order underneath the seeming chaos, just as in the depths of the ocean there is a quiescence that is undisturbed by the play of waves at the surface. Quiescence may be another way of talking about boundlessness.

Shunyata, then, carries and permeates all phenomena and makes their development possible. Shunyata is often equated with the "absolute" in Mahayana, since it is without duality and beyond empirical forms. In quantum physics, ultimate reality is equated with formless energy at the core of each atom. For the Buddha, dependent origination was the ultimate reality of all forms. Energy (in physics) or shunyata (in Mahayana Buddhism) is not a state of mere nothingness but is the very source of all life precisely because of its inherent dynamism.

Another helpful way to understand shunyata is through the Zen term "nowness," sometimes used interchangeably with "momentariness." In the absence of a permanent, abiding substance anywhere, there is only the nowness of things: ephemeral, transitory, momentary. This nowness is all there is. *How* things are is *what* they are. In traditional Buddhist literature, the nowness of things is described as *tathata*, or "suchness." The Mahayana elaboration of the notion of *tathata* suggested that when the futility of all conceptualized thinking is recognized, reality is experienced as pure "suchness." What is realized in suchness is the existence of form-as-itself (the treeness of the tree, for instance), but this realization is suffused with an intuitive wisdom (*prajna*) that sees a form as momentary and essentially lacking (*shunya*) in any abiding substance. Masao Abe, among others, insists that "Emptiness is Suchness."

A positive understanding of suchness is nonseparation. If all manifestations lack an abiding substance, they all share that fundamental "lack." The logic of this lack is that there is no difference, at the core, between one thing and another. They all share the constructive-generative processes of dependent arising and momentary manifestation. If there is no difference in these basic processes, how can any separation be made except at the most superficial level? In the great ocean the wave and the water cannot be separated from each other; the wave is the water, and water is the wave.

The first vow a Zen practitioner takes in formal practice is "Beings are numberless, I vow to free them," which is sometimes phrased in this form: "All beings, one body; I vow to liberate." It means all sentient beings share the same one "body" or the commonality of dependent origination. To bring one person to liberation is to simultaneously impact the liberation process of all beings everywhere.

Anagarika Govinda uses the word *transparency* to come to a fuller understanding of shunyata:

If *sunyata* hints at the nonsubstantiality of the world and the interrelationship of all beings and things, then there can be no better word to describe its meaning than *transparency*. This word avoids the pitfalls of a pure negation and replaces the concepts of substance, resistance, impenetrability, limitation, and materiality with something that can be experienced and is closely related to the concepts of space and light.[23]

He goes on to elaborate,

Far from being the expression of a nihilistic philosophy which denies all reality, it (*sunyata*) is the logical consequence of the *anatman* (non-self) doctrine of nonsubstantiality. *Sunyata* is the emptiness of all conceptual designations and at the same time the recognition of a higher, incommensurable and indefinable reality, which can be experienced only in the state of perfect enlightenment.

While we are able to come to an understanding of relativity by way of reasoning, the experience of universality and completeness can be attained only when all conceptual thought, all word-thinking, has come to rest. The realization of the teachings of the *Prajna-paramita Sutra* can come about only on the path of meditative practice (*yogachara*), through a transformation of our consciousness. Meditation in this sense is, therefore, no more a search after intellectual solutions or an analysis of worldly phenomena with worldly means—which would merely be moving around in circles—but a breaking out from this circle, an abandoning of our thought-habits in order to "reach the other shore" (as it has been said not only in the ancient *Prajna-paramita-hridaya*, but also in the ancient *Sutta Nipata* of the Pali Canon.) This requires a complete reversal of our outlook, a complete spiritual transformation or, as the Lankavatara Sutra expresses it, "a turning about in the deepest seat of our consciousness." This reversal brings about a new spiritual outlook, similar to that which the Buddha experienced when returning from the Tree of Enlightenment. A new dimension of consciousness is being opened by this experience, which transcends the limits of mundane thought.[24]

…five skandhas are…

The Sanskrit word *skandha* (Pali: *khandha*) literally means "a group," "a heap," or "an aggregate." In the Buddhist understanding the five skandhas are the "heaps" of form, feelings, perceptions, impulses, and consciousness, and are taken to constitute the entirety of what is generally known as "self" or "personality." There's a twofold understanding of the aggregates in the Buddhist tradition: as groups of existence and as groups of clinging. In the first understanding, they are descriptive of the psychophysical personality; in the second, they are also descriptive but in a cautionary sense as doorways leading to clinging. Whether they are being used in the first or the second understanding will depend on the context. The Buddha called these five skandhas *nama-rupa*, meaning "name and form," or the psychophysical. The invitation of the Buddha is to examine these factors of existence, not analytically but in terms of their relational structure. Such an examination reveals that each of these skandhas depends on conditions for its manifestation, and each depends on its relational structures with the other four to gain the vitality and power it has in our life. No factor in the set enjoys the self-sufficiency to be the sole attribute of an assumed "I." The statement that "all five skandhas are empty" is the bedrock of Buddhist teachings. A detailed look at them will expand our understanding of shunyata.

The first and the most obvious of the skandhas is *rupa*, physical form or the body. In other usages in Buddhist languages, *rupa* also means materiality. Form includes all the tangibles—mass, weight, solidity, color, shape—as well as organs for sight, smell, taste, hearing, and touch. The corporeality of form provides material support for the four nonmaterial skandhas of sensations, perception, formation, and consciousness in the psychophysical conglomeration. A metaphor often used to describe the relationship of form to the other four skandhas is that of water contained in a vessel; form is the vessel; the other four are like the water contained in the vessel. Admittedly, this metaphor works only so far, but the basic idea is there.

In quantum physics a form or a phenomenon (particle) is seen to be devoid of any solid, everlasting substance. The form is held together in time and space by the underlying energy interacting in a certain pattern and balance. All skandhas, whether physical or mental, share four temporal characteristics: arising, stabilizing, decaying, and dissolving. "Stabilization" takes place on the upswing of a coalescing energy movement; decay and dissolution occur on the downward swing of the same movement, when the balance in which the elements have been held together momentarily loses its inner tension and the organism is left with insufficient vitality to hold itself in time and space. It is important to keep in mind that all these changes are taking place in extremely rapid sequence; at the molecular level, they can be discerned only through a microscope.

Today we understand from scientific research that the human body operates through chemical and molecular processes. By their very nature these processes are in a state of constant, even chaotic change at the cellular level. As mentioned earlier, millions of cells are born and die in each passing second. There's no solidity at the core. But in our ignorance we live as if the body were solid and unchanging at its core.

The poet W. H. Auden has said, "Our claim to own our bodies and our world / is our catastrophe."[25] How can we claim ownership of something that's constantly changing? What does it tell us about the nature of the claim? A deluded mind believes a manifestation to be a thing-in-itself, whereas Buddhist teachings point out that a manifestation is an event. A thing is perceived by the deluded mind to be solid and self-abiding; an event is seen by a mind informed by prajna as a resultant outcome of a certain process. To see oneself truly and authentically, as an *event*—an ever-changing process—rather than a thing-in-itself is the greatest act of re-imaging.

What is true of the human body is also true of all other phenomena in the universe. All are undergoing constant change in each nanosecond. The tallest mountains are changing at their subatomic level, even though such change may be measurable only by the most sophisticated of instruments. The changes in the autumn leaf—first its color, then its fall from the limb, then desiccation and disintegration—are visible to the naked eye, but its cellular changes at the quantum level are essentially no different from those of the great mountain.

In his commentary on the Heart Sutra, Red Pine makes the important distinction that "the word rupa does not actually refer to a concrete object but to the appearance of an object. Form is like a mask that cannot be removed without revealing its own illusory identity. Such a mask might be worn by a table or a sunset or a number or a coin... or a universe. Whether such things are real is not relevant. The important thing is that they make up a presumed outside to a presumed inside."[26]

The skandha called feeling (*vedana*) is the general designation for feeling tone and sensations. It is perhaps more useful to translate it as *sensation*, since *feeling* in Western languages tends to obscure and psychologize the issue. It is clear from a close reading of the Pali canon that the Buddha's intention in using the word *vedana* was to offer a phenomenological description of the experience rather than something psychological. Indeed, there are Buddhist teachers who insist on translating this Pali/Sanskrit term as *sensation* rather than *feeling*.

The word *vedana* comes from the root verb *vid*, "to know" or "to experience." In this sense, it is an evaluation of an object with which awareness comes into contact. The spectrum of such objects is practically unlimited, for awareness comes into contact not only with material forms but also with thoughts, emotions, psychological constructs, and so forth. Vedana is a response to or evaluation of such contacts, and is classified into pleasant, unpleasant, and neutral. This response is almost always a complex mix of passive and active.

As with the skandha of material form, sensations arise as a result of factors coming together. They then gain in intensity, maintain it for some period, then lose the tension, and finally disappear. Sensations arise and pass away in nanoseconds but can be accessed in a state of deep and focused meditation. A particular sensation will change into another sensation, which in turn will change *ad infinitum*. Sensations are an inevitable part of a living organism. All living beings everywhere experience these sensations in their own species-specific way. Vedana provides the affective tone of particular experiences.

The skandha called perception (Pali: *sañña*; Skt: *samjna*) includes apprehension of form, sound, smell, taste, touch and bodily impressions, and mental objects. Its function is noting and identifying. It supplies the framework that allows us to generate the affective tone in our comprehension (our perception of the snake is different from our perception of the sunflower, so the two generate very different affective tones).

Recent advances in cognitive science allow us to understand this Buddhist term also as "cognition"; hence, perception-cognition is a better translation of sañña. Perception-cognition takes place only in relation to an object (or thought) and does not exist independently of an object of attention. Moreover, it takes place within an observing consciousness; hence it is impossible to separate the subjectivity of an observing consciousness from the particular manner in which an object is observed. Today's advanced research in psychological testing shows that no two people observe the same object in exactly the same manner.

The skandha called impulse (Pali: *sankhara*; Skt: *samskara*) refers to formations or constructions. It is also at times translated as volition or predisposition, or even "memory." It is one of the crucial words in Buddhist teachings. The Abhidhamma-pitaka, the traditional compendium of Buddhist psychology, lists fifty-two sankharas including volition, attention, discrimination, joy, happiness, equanimity, resolve, effort, compulsion, and concentration; included in this skandha are all the volitional impulses or intentions that precede an action. These intentions themselves are formed by a residual memory in the background, which supplies templates that the faculty of perception-cognition applies to forms and sensations that awareness contacts.

Since actions can be physical, verbal, or mental, formations can accordingly be physical, verbal, or mental. This skandha refers both to the activity of forming and the passive state of being formed. These formations or constructions are the impressions, tendencies, and residual possibilities in one's consciousness, and are the sum total of one's personality. They are the totality of one's actions and thoughts in the past, including those of earlier births. In this sense, these formations are karmic conditions for future rebirth. If no formations or imprints are present in one's consciousness—none from the past and none in the present—no karma will be produced and no further birth takes place. Since the imprints can be positive, negative, or neutral, they determine the type of rebirth that will take place, since their quality conditions consciousness, and through them consciousness seeks a form in rebirth to manifest those qualities. (This is, of course, only a rudimentary explanation of Buddha's teaching on karma and rebirth.)

Today, it is possible to understand sankhara in psychological terms as referring to all the unconscious residues and imprints in consciousness. Imprints at the unconscious level inform our unconscious intentional processes; and even though we may believe that we are forming an autonomous intention in each instance, the roots of the intention sink deep in the unconscious.

Sankhara provides the volitional and emotive elements of apprehension. It should also be noted that the Buddhist understanding of sankhara as partially unconscious is not always congruous with the contemporary, especially Freudian, understanding of the unconscious. This is not the place to detail their differences. Suffice it to note that the Buddhist understanding of sankharas needs to be engaged on its own ground rather than through the prism of Freudian psychology.

The skandha called consciousness (Pali: *viññana*; Skt: *vijnana*) is the faculty of knowing or the basic awareness in the totality of experience. Consciousness has one of the six sense organs (eyes, ears, nose, tongue, body, and mind) as its basis and one of the six corresponding phenomena (visual form, sound, smell, taste, touch, and thought) as its object. Consciousness arises out of contact between the object and the corresponding organ, but consciousness does not recognize an object itself. It is only an awareness of the presence of an object. For instance, when eye comes into contact with a blue color, eye-consciousness simply "sees" the presence of a dark area (as opposed to a bright area). The recognition that the dark area is not merely "a color" but, say, dark *blue* comes from the skandha of perception-cognition. Likewise, the hearing-consciousness only hears the sound but does not recognize the category of sound; this is done by the perception-cognition aggregate, and so on. The basic framework of the working of consciousness was laid down by the Buddha in an early text called the Chachakka Sutta (Six Sets of Six; Majjhima Nikaya, sutta 148).

A common mistake about consciousness is to misunderstand it (in secular terms) as some sort of engine that drives the car, or (in religious terms) a soul or permanent self that remains unchanged and autonomous despite all the changes in the corporeal form. In both (mis)understandings, there is an assumption of something substantial that remains unchanged in time and space. The Buddha taught that consciousness arises only out of *conditions*; without the presence of such conditions there is no consciousness. Consciousness depends on form, feelings, perceptions, and impulses for its arising and cannot exist independently of them. In other words, there is no "consciousness" independent of *nama-rupa*, the psychophysical system we have been talking about. In the Buddha's teachings, it is essentially an observing function. The metaphor here is that of a cloud: the cloud appears as a result of atmospheric conditions but has no independent existence; its appearing and disappearing are entirely dependent on conditions.

The central problem of human existence, in Buddhist understanding, is the problem of a "self" occupying an unchanging, permanent relation to phenomena. The problem is twofold: the first is how the "self" sees itself—through linguistic, emotional, and intellectual matrixes; the second is how it understands each psychological or physiological phenomenon it comes into contact with through these same matrixes.

This relationship always posits the self in relationship to an "other," and it is practically impossible to understand the "self" without this

"other" because the self is always defining itself through its own individuating *relationality*. This individuating or selfing is premised on sep-
arating itself from everything else, including causes and conditions, and
on seeing itself as autonomous and self-validating. Religions compound
the problem by proposing to see the individual as an entity with an
essence or a soul that abides unchangingly in time and space. The soul
theory plays itself out in different ways in monotheistic and polytheis-
tic religions, but the revolution of the Buddha in his own culture was to
investigate the matter of self and not find any abiding existent.

A great many misunderstandings have taken place in interpreting the
Buddha's teaching of *anatta* or non-self, but it is important to keep in
mind that while the Buddha pointed to a lack of an abiding core, he did
not deny an existential personality. In other words, things exist but they
are not real. For the Buddha the individual or the personality was a con-
glomerate of five aggregates or heaps—skandhas—as we have been discussing. In and of themselves, these aggregates are a biological or
phenomenological system, and out of their interplay a sense of self is
born. The following chart may help in giving visual expression to what
is meant here:

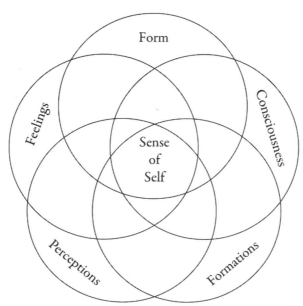

The challenge of Buddhist thought and practice is to recognize and separate the sense of self from all assumptions and notions about a permanent, autonomous self. A *sense* of self is vastly different from a *belief* in a solid, unchanging self. A sense of self is quite acceptable as a routine existential process embedded in brain structures and linguistic usage. It is not a theological issue. Any discussion of "the self," on the other hand, becomes a theological discussion sooner rather than later.

As mentioned earlier, these five aggregates are "aggregates of clinging" in that the reified self claims ownership of these aggregates individually and collectively. In both modalities craving or desire attaches itself to these five aggregates and turns them into objects of attachment, thus creating suffering. When examined closely, the workings of the five skandhas constitute a feedback loop that gets more and more elaborate in its self-referentiality.

When the self is seen in this way—as a sense of self, a momentary process rather than an entity—it follows that the "self" of each and every phenomenon in the universe is also likewise constructed. All phenomena are dependently arisen; they too follow the trajectory of generation, stabilization, decay, and dissolution, with no abiding core or substance. It is only when we have an illusion of "the self" as a separate entity that we create "the other." Both "self" and "other" are acts of imagination—a distorted image, for sure, and one that has disturbing consequences.

To put it another way, dualistic thinking creates competing paradigms: good creates evil and vice versa; "the I" creates "the you" and vice versa; being creates nonbeing and vice versa.

This problem of self and other is summed up quite elegantly in perhaps the best-known phrase from the medieval Japanese Zen master Dogen in his *Shobogenzo*: "To study the buddha way is to study the self. To study the self is to forget the self. To forget the self is to be actualized by myriad things."[27]

This is a holistic paradigm: when the self is not creating the self, it is also not creating the myriad things of the universe apart from the self. Only in that transparency of nothing-being-created is it possible for the self to be awakened by the ten thousand things of the world, because only then does it see its own face in each of those myriad things. That transparency would be impossible if the self were to create itself and the other as two separate entities. Just as the self sees itself as a transitory phenomenon, so does it see each of the ten thousand things of the world; there is no separation in its perception-cognition, and hence there is an awakening to the nonseparation of self and the other.

On close examination we find each of the aggregates to be a construction put into place by a nexus of causes and conditions. A construct, by definition, is not real in itself because it exists as an *effect* of causes and conditions. That it can also operate as a causal factor for other effects does not endow it with an own-being or self-nature (*svabhava*) or an inalienable core. The construct has a certain shape, like a swelling or a bubble, while it exists as an effect, but this shape is only momentary and will change when the underlying causes and conditions change.

The aggregates are to be understood in terms of their relational structures; their existence depends on causes and conditions. In isolation, none of them achieves any degree of self-sufficiency. As a matrix, they all together attain a momentary validity but not substantiality. The matrix may extend beyond the local—temporally and spatially—but does not suggest the stability of the local.

On our television screens these days we see satellite pictures of hurricanes as they march across oceans and continents. We put a name on the hurricane and describe its strength and speed, and it's easy enough to imagine that this hurricane is a solid entity. But it's clear from the satellite pictures that the hurricane is constantly changing and shifting; its course is unpredictable and the time of its ripping through an area uncertain. Numerous causes and conditions affect the hurricane's path and manifestation. Its reality is that of a process undergoing continual change with no abiding core.

Each of the five aggregates is like this; all phenomena in the universe undergo this process. Thus the world of samsara is a shadow play of appearance and change, generation and conversion, nothing solid, nothing abiding. And yet like the hurricane it has tremendous power to do damage.

...and is saved from all suffering and distress.

What follows from the above is that when we understand the aggregates as processes without independent existence, we are not anguished by their dissolution. Formation and dissolution is the natural order of things. There cannot be ownership of attributes within a process since all attributes are themselves processes caused by processes nestled into processes. It is in this sense that the Heart Sutra and the Prajna Paramita traditions describe the five skandhas as empty.

All suffering is caused by delusion—misperception as to the nature of self and phenomena. Because of this delusion we cling to things, claim ownership of them, don't want to let them go. The Buddha's proposal for liberation from suffering is simple enough: understand the true nature of phenomena—including the self—and don't cling to anything. This non-clinging will eventually lead to serenity, contentment, and joy in life.

It is the ego that clings to the deluded view of a permanent self and distorts the nature of reality. In deep meditation, one bypasses the deceptive filters created by the ego and realizes, on a direct, experiential level, that the five skandhas are mere processes and that no self exists in the sense of a permanent, eternal, integral, independent substance. Through this realization a person is saved from deluded views and the pain and suffering that ensue.

Shariputra, form does not differ from emptiness; emptiness does not differ from form. That which is form is emptiness, that which is emptiness is form.

This is the most provocative statement in the sutra, and arguably in the entire Mahayana philosophy. We have established above the basic understanding that all phenomena, all existents, lack any inherent self-abiding substance (again, *svabhava*). This lack of a self-abiding substance has been shown through the principle of dependent arising. This lack is the essential feature of each and every form. Each form carries within itself an intimation of its own lack/emptiness.

The sutra insists that form is emptiness. There is a critical difference between form being *empty* and form being *emptiness*. As we have been discussing, in the Prajna Paramita sutras shunyata—or its correlate, depending arising—are the ultimate nature of phenomena. At the same time, this emptiness does not exist apart from phenomena but permeates and indeed comprises each and every phenomenon. Therefore, shunyata cannot be sought as a thing-in-itself apart from the totality of all forms. And although all forms are informed at their core by an inherent lack, or shunyata, this does not negate the conventional appearance of form. In this sense emptiness can be known only conceptually, and any conception is dependent upon the form it qualifies, as much as the form is dependent on emptiness for its qualification. Thus form is emptiness and emptiness is form; at its core level, form cannot be differentiated from emptiness, nor can emptiness be differentiated from form.

It must be said that the linguistic formulation of these two lines in the Sanskrit version of the Heart Sutra—"Iha Sariputra rupam sunyata sunyataiva rupam, rupam na prithak sunyata sunyataya na prithag rupam, yad rupam sa sunyata ya sunyata tad rupam" has created unnecessary problems for later generations. If the phrase *rupam sunyata* ("form is emptiness") had been formulated as *rupam sunya* ("form is empty [of own-being]"), we would perhaps have had a more accurate reflection of what is meant here. We would also have been spared a lot of theorizing. In the appendix to this book I have done a playful rewriting of the Heart Sutra that replaces the conventional juxtaposition of form and emptiness. The aim of this rewrite is to capture the urgency of lack of own-being without getting caught in the metaphysical theories of emptiness that dominate contemporary discussions about this core Mahayana teaching.

In Western languages, "form is empty" reads entirely differently from "form is emptiness." It is a problem of grammatical parts of speech, and this problem extends throughout our contemporary engagements with Buddhist teachings. In the understanding of these teachings that we now possess, we can say with some assurance that they are about processes, not things; as such, their authentic meaning derives from "verbing," that is to say, their status as verbs rather than nouns. This means that if all of Buddha's teachings were to be understood as verbs rather than nouns, as qualities rather than entities, we would be in a much better position to understand their relevance in our transformational process.

Take for example the Pali word *anatta*. In the last two hundred years, much frustration has been expressed in trying to understand it as "no-self." This linguistic formulation automatically posits a noun (no-self) against another noun (self). But if the same term is translated as "non-self" or "not-self," it becomes a "verbing" statement and avoids the problematic "nouning."

A "nouning" formulation identifies phenomena as things, as entities, and understands its properties as a subset of entities and things, to an infinite regress. But a "verbing" orientation—"selfing" and "emptying"—goes a long way toward getting a grasp on Buddha's process-based phenomenological approach to all forms of existence. "Nouning" leads to conceptual and metaphysical statements, and these invite metaphysical counterstatements (self and no-self in our current discussion), which in turn invite metaphysical counter-counterstatements, and so on to absurd lengths.

It should be clear that this core statement of the sutra is not a metaphysical statement about "emptiness" but rather a straightforward assertion that each form is identical not only with its own lack (of svabhava, or own-being) but also with the lack of all forms in the universe.

At the same time it is not a nihilistic negation of form or a reifying assertion of emptiness. Rather, it is simply about "seeing things as they are"—lacking any inherent existence at their core but fully vibrant in their manifestation. Understand that one is the other, that they are two descriptions of the same thing, and you understand the core reality of each and every thing in the phenomenal world. And so we come to the classic Middle Way of the Buddha—the creative dynamism between negation and assertion.

The same is true of feelings, perceptions, impulses, consciousness.

The lack of own-being/*svabhava* does not negate the conventional appearance of feelings/sensations, perceptions, impulses, and consciousness. All of these skandhas are constantly manifesting and dissolving in a complex and fascinating manner as a result of causal conditions. These conditions are, in turn, empty of any core and are conditioned by other sets of conditions which, too, are empty, and so on. All conditions qualifying other conditions qualifying the skandhas are momentary phenomena giving rise to momentary phenomena. None of these has any inherent self-nature; all are constructions; all are processes.

Shariputra, all dharmas are marked with emptiness.

Dharma is a comprehensive term in the Hindu and Buddhist traditions with a variety of meanings and applications at multiple levels. In the sutra here the term is used in the sense of a fundamental unit of existence. *Dharmas* are the building blocks of the phenomenal world, including the five aggregates of the mind-body system we have been investigating. They are analogous to the atoms of Democritus or the monads of Leibniz. It seems that this is how the Abhidhamma philosophers saw ultimate reality and, on the basis of this understanding, constructed their systems of explication.

As we have seen, the Mahayana teaching of shunyata challenged this Abhidhamma understanding. The Mahayana perspective, like the original orientation of the Buddha, seeks a middle way between nihilism and substantialism, between denial and assertion. The term "point-instant" perhaps comes closest to recapturing the insight behind the term *dharma* within the context of the Heart Sutra. A "point-instant" has minuscule extension in space and practically no duration. The analogy of wave-particle unpredictability of quantum physics best captures the drama of "point-instants."

The Abhidhamma understanding is that the skandhas are made from these fundamental units, the dhammas/dharmas. The Mahayana critique of this notion is that it lends itself easily to dharmas being some kind of primeval *stuff*. This is, in a way, analogous to Newton's physics. In the Heart Sutra understanding, dharmas themselves are not solid objects positioned in time and space, just as waves and particles in quantum physics equations are not. The dharmas are point-instants that make a momentary appearance [as skandhas] and then flicker out.

The relationship between a dharma and a skandha is that of between the cause and the effect. The dharma of an inflated balloon is the air that has been pumped into it. In and of itself, the air in the inflated balloon is not a thing, but the air provides vitality to the manifestation of that particular form, in this case an inflated balloon. Air has a certain tension that maintains the form of balloon, but it cannot be grasped or held on to. Similarly, all dharmas everywhere, since the beginning of all processes, exhibit similar characteristics—building blocks of skandhas but nothing in themselves; they are empty of any abiding core or duration. There is absolutely nothing one can hold on to.

In other words, Mahayana offers a nonsubstantialist position as a counterpoint to the seemingly substantialist theory of dharmas in the Abhidharma. As has been mentioned above, the substantialist position may have arisen as a misreading of the Abhidhamma philosophers, who may not have had this view in mind.

They do not appear or disappear, are not tainted or pure, do not increase or decrease.

The quality of appearing or disappearing is usually attributed, in our misperceptions, to what we take to be solid objects. If the dharmas are the animating principle of an endless series of momentary flickerings, point-instants, they cannot be invested with the quality of appearing or disappearing precisely because neither the animating principle nor the flickerings are solid objects. Again, the wave-particle equation in quantum physics is helpful here. Neither wave nor particle is an "appearing" or a "disappearing" of anything solid. Both are momentary flickerings—point-instants—of the underlying quantum energy. A flickering, an expression of quantum energy extremely swift in time and minuscule in space, is not in itself tainted or pure, nor does it increase or decrease.

A helpful analogy here may be that of waves in the ocean. A large wave is not a distinct entity but is composed of a series of smaller waves which in turn are composed of still smaller waves and so on. Behind the illusion of a "wave" is a remarkably swift movement of molecules of water in patterns. A wave does not exist in the ocean as an individuated, autonomous entity. There's a manifestation called "a wave," but it's a flickering point-instant, just like the flickering of a candle flame in a gentle breeze. Out of ignorance we may consider certain qualities (appearing/disappearing, taint/purity, increase/decrease) as inherent in conventional appearances (in skandhas), but since, at the core of conventional appearances, these are only unpredictable flickerings (dharmas), our reification of these qualities as "real-in-themselves" is a deluded view. The only place where our deluded view will find resolution is through resting in the paradox of ultimate lack and conventional appearance of forms. This resting place is to be accessed through deep meditation rather than some dry, abstract cogitation.

In science the "animating" principle of gravity is inviolate, but it cannot be grasped, does not appear or disappear, is neither pure nor tainted, and so on. The categories of arising and disappearing, pure and impure, and increasing or decreasing are dualistic categories. They belong to our habits of affirmation and negation which are, in turn, produced by our conceptual thinking. These conceptual constructs are not integral to core quantum energy or the lack of svabhava in phenomena.

In a deep meditative state one transcends these habit patterns of affirmation or negation. One touches the shunyata of things but does not engage in linguistic and conceptual categories of affirmation or negation, holy or unholy, and so on. Here it would be wise to remind ourselves of Nagarjuna's caution that, as a concept, shunyata too is empty. Any affirmation or negation of shunyata would be conceptual and hence deluded.

So, since the defining characteristics of all dharmas is their emptiness or shunyata, they cannot be purified, nor can they be defiled. They also cannot increase or decrease. A Zen poem by the contemporary Korean Zen master Seung Sahn confirms this as one of the great insights of Buddhist practice:

> Good and evil have no self-nature;
> Holy and unholy are empty names;
> In front of the [sense] door is the land of stillness and light;
> Spring comes, grass grows by itself.[28]

Purification or defilement, coming or going, increasing or decreasing—all conceptual dualities have no home in the emptiness of the dharmas.

Therefore, in emptiness no form, no feelings, perceptions, impulses, consciousness. No eyes, no ears, no nose, no tongue, no body, no mind, no color, no sound, no smell, no taste, no touch, no object of mind, no realm of eyes, and so forth until no realm of mind-consciousness.

This passage is a further refutation of the earlier assertions by the Abhidharmists with regard to skandhas and dharmas. Not wishing the hearer to somehow form the impression that "emptiness is form" or any such category of analysis, the sutra now employs the classical Indian philosophical methodology of negation. This methodology is two-pronged; on the one hand, it denies any identification of shunyata with the skandhas (form, feelings, perceptions, impulses, consciousness) or six sense organs (eyes, ears, nose, tongue, body, mind) or the phenomena perceived by the sense organs (shape, sound, smell, taste, touch, or thought) or the six consciousnesses produced as a result of contact between the sense organs and the external phenomena (eye consciousness, ear consciousness, nose consciousness, tongue consciousness, touch consciousness, mind consciousness). This negation is a rejection of the Abhidharmist predilection for numerous categories of analysis. The point is that all these categories and their descriptions are linguistic and conceptual categories; in themselves they are empty of svabhava, and are being emptied out in each moment; there is no solidity called "emptiness" that can be attributed to them.

On the other hand, the sutra asserts that the principle of shunyata—synonymous with dependent origination—is ineffable and inexpressible, and is not to be confounded with eye, ear, nose, tongue, and so on. This deconstructive process continues until all categories are denied as identifiable with shunyata.

Therefore, in shunyata there is nothing to hold on to. Shunyata is complete absence or lack of a core in all phenomena, yet it is not nihilistically void. Zen master Bojo Chinul (1158–1210), the founder of Korean Zen, makes a forceful argument in this regard:

> At that place, sounds and discriminations do not take place... This is the life force of all the buddhas and patriarchs—have no further doubt about that. Since it has no former shape, how can it be large or small? Since it cannot be large or small, how can it have limitations? Since it has no limitations, it cannot have inside or outside. Since there is no inside or outside, there is no far or near. As there is no far or near, there is no here and there. As there is no here or there, there is no coming or going. As there is no coming or going, there is no birth or death. As there is no birth or death, there is no past or present. As there is no past or present, there is no delusion or awakening. As there is no delusion or awakening, there is no ordinary man or saint. As there is no ordinary man or saint, there is no purity or impurity. Since there is no impurity or purity, there is no right or wrong. Since there is no right or wrong, names and words do not apply to it. Since none of these concepts apply, all sense-bases and sense-objects, all deluded thoughts, even forms and shapes and names and words are inapplicable. Hence how can it be anything but originally void and calm and originally no-thing?
>
> Nevertheless, at that point where all dharmas are empty, the numinous awareness is not obscured. It is not the same as insentience, for its nature is spiritually deft. This is your pure mind-essence of void and calm, numinous awareness.[29]

For Chinul, this deconstructed space is "numinous awareness." For other Zen masters, this is a place of radical nondiscrimination; for the Buddha, this is a place of radical non-clinging. For quantum physicists, this is the place of dynamically pulsating energy at the core of each form. In an insight into shunyata there is a letting go of all categories of

analysis, all conceptual constructs that allow the ego to cling to "self."
When one transcends the rationality of Abhidhamma thinking and
enters the realm of intuitive truth, only then does one come face to face
with the qualityless, valueless, ineffable shunyata taught by the
Mahayana tradition.

No ignorance and also no extinction of it, and so forth until no old age and death and also no extinction of them.

This passage is one more deconstruction of the sequence of causal links as enumerated in the second noble truth of dependent arising. What the sutra is rejecting here is not the principle of dependent arising but rather the scholastic claim made by the Abhidharmists that the twelve links of dependent arising must always operate in the same sequence, either forward (as in the second noble truth) or backward (as in the third noble truth). Once again, this statement is less an example of waywardness in the sutra than of intra-Buddhist debates going on in early medieval India.

The legend of Buddha's awakening tells us that during the first watch of the night of his great awakening, he experienced all his past lives, one by one, as he had lived them. In the second watch of the night, he witnessed the death and rebirth of all universes, and all beings in them, across the eons. Still, to his credit, he was not convinced that he had discovered the root cause of human suffering, as he had set out to do when he took his great vow not to move from his seat under the tree. Finally, at dawn, he saw the morning star and in a flash understood what he had been seeking. This insight has been articulated in later tradition as *pratitya-samutpada*, the chain of dependent origination, and presented as a schema:

> There is ignorance/delusion (Pali: *avijja*; Skt: *avidya*) [in each moment's apprehension by the self as to the true nature of phenomena it is encountering].

> Ignorance leads to mental formations or impulses (Pali: *sankhara*; Skt: *samskara*).

> Impulses or mental formations give rise to a state of consciousness (*vinnana*; *vijnana*), the totality of thoughts, speech, and actions.

Consciousness determines how the resulting mental and physical phenomena (*nama-rupa* or the realm of name and form) works.

Mental and physical phenomena condition the six sense realms (*salayatana*; *shadayatana*): the five physical sense organs of eye, ear, nose, tongue, and body, plus the mind.

The six sense realms come into contact (*phassa*; *sparsha*) with [sensorial and mental] phenomena.

Contact gives rise to sensations or feelings (*vedana*).

Feelings or sensations give rise to thirst or craving (*tanha*; *trishna*).

Craving gives rise to clinging (*upadana*).

Clinging leads to becoming (*bhava*).

Becoming leads to rebirth (*jati*).

Rebirth leads to suffering, old age, and death (*jara-marana*; *jara-maranam*) in a new cycle

Often this chain of dependent origination is graphically represented as a circle and variously called the Wheel of Samsara, the Wheel of Becoming, or the Wheel of Karma. The Buddha taught that the turning of this wheel could be brought to a stop, to a cessation—through the complete cessation of ignorance, mental formations are eradicated; through the eradication of mental formations, consciousness is re-formed, and so forth until one arrives at the cessation of conditioned rebirth, and hence of suffering, old age, and death. This stopping of the turning of the wheel of suffering is often called "turning the Wheel of Dharma" and is called the path to nirvana, the state of being in which all deluded views about anything permanent or substantial in human existence are eradicated.

It is important to bear in mind that each of the twelve factors in the chain of dependent origination is a conditioned effect as well as a conditioning agent. Each is both a cause and a result. As such, they are all interdependent, and no single factor is absolute or independent. Each factor is a process rather than a thing, and as such inherently empty. When the Wheel of Dharma is turned, all these factors find their resolution in the deconstructive processes of nirvana or shunyata.

The argument of the Heart Sutra is that the twelve links do not always move causally in the same sequence. To assume they always do is to impose an artificial condition on both the meditative and the liberative experience. Instead, the metaphor could be of a bubbling pot of soup in which the twelve links of dependent arising inform one another in unpredictable ways.

This passage in the sutra also continues the earlier argument that none of the twelve links has the self-sufficiency to stand alone. In shunyata understanding, as noted earlier, forms are only flickerings—without any quality of solidity or time duration—manifesting themselves momentarily. Knowing this fundamental truth, we are spared the necessity of categorizing the insights of the Buddha. Mahayana tradition insists that it is enough for a follower to firmly hold on to the thought of enlightenment and practice diligently. A firm belief that in shunyata all things find their resolution is therefore enough for a Mahayana believer. To know through the eye of prajna that all the twelve links in the chain of dependent origination are interconnected and interrelated is to echo the words of Werner Heisenberg, one of the founders of quantum physics: "The world thus appears as a complicated tissue of events, in which connections of different kinds alternate or overlap or combine and thereby determine the texture of the whole."[30]

No suffering, no origination, no stopping, no path, no cognition, also no attainment with nothing to attain.

This passage applies the same deconstructive approach to the four noble truths as the previous line did to the twelve links of dependent arising. We cannot help but speculate how controversial this passage and the preceding one must have been in ancient or early medieval India, rejecting, as they seem to do, the framework of the four noble truths as a way to think about enlightenment. The Buddhist orthodoxy of the time had insisted that the four noble truths had to be accepted as an unquestionable scriptural authority. The four noble truths is the first teaching the Buddha ever gave (to his five former ascetic colleagues) soon after his enlightenment. It is called the Discourse on Turning the Wheel of Dharma (Dhamma-cakka-pavatana Sutta). In this schema, the four noble truths are:

> Conditioned existence is *dukkha* (pain, suffering, discomfort, disease, sense of incompleteness).
>
> *Dukkha* is caused by "thirst" or craving (Pali/Skr: *tanha*), the desire to be, desire to have.
>
> The thirst can be stopped (*nirodha*).
>
> It can be stopped by walking the eightfold path (wholesome view, wholesome intention, wholesome speech, wholesome action, wholesome livelihood, wholesome effort, wholesome mindfulness, wholesome concentration).

The Mahayana disciples had no quarrel with the insight contained in any of these truths or steps, but what precipitated a conflict for them was the Abhidhamma tendency to freeze each of these four noble truths into an "ultimate," which converted it into a polemic of "holy" and "absolute." This polemic was joined to the orthodox establishment's insistence that the monastic elite was the sole custodian of the Buddha's teachings and that the elite's interpretations were incontrovertible.

Through the innovation of shunyata as the ontological and transcendent nature of reality, the Mahayana followers declared all categories—and all interpretations of them—to be dualistic, and thus inapplicable. By arguing for a simple faith in the thought of enlightenment and diligent practice, these Mahayana followers sought to make the vitality of Buddha's enlightenment experience available to any and all, laypersons and monastics alike.

This passage then is a declaration that suffering, the origination of suffering, and the stopping of suffering by following a certain path are, when they are employed as linguistic devices, themselves empty categories. They may have their use as a road map, but their classificatory schema must not become a self-validating principle. In the prajna-wisdom of shunyata, all sequentials and consequentials, all causal schemas, dissolve; there cannot be any notion of "suffering" as some monolithic entity that exists by itself. Suffering is a subjectively designated experience. The Buddhist understanding of suffering (as distinct from pain or discomfort) is that it is a psychologically induced notion that need not necessarily be imposed on an actual experience. That being the case, there is no distinction between suffering and the end of suffering; what has arisen and what has passed away are episodes of mental labeling.

The basic argument here is that the Buddha's teachings are not about the sanctity or holiness of this map or that map; they are about the nature of experience itself. This is a radical idea. Because of our conditioning, we depend on a road map if we want to go somewhere. The Mahayana innovators had no quarrel with this basic wish, but they pointed out that, more often than not, the map gets mistaken for the path. In other words, what was important for them was moving into the experience that lies outside our clouded, deluded thinking. If the map or the path becomes an obstacle rather than a help, it should be abandoned.

The implication is that an experience of cessation (*nirodha*) can be obtained without necessarily following the eightfold path in a *regimented* order.

It must be added here that at the experiential level, there would be no serious disagreement among Theravada and Mahayana practitioners about the experience of cessation itself. In the sutra the Mahayana innovators are simply and consciously moving away from the doctrinal primacy of earlier articulations.

The sutra declares, almost ruthlessly, that there is no cognition or attainment because there is nothing "out there" to cognize or attain. If spiritual knowledge is reduced to textual knowledge or textual learning, it goes against the spirit of everything the Buddha was trying to convey. His own awakening experience was not a result of anything he had been told or had read but was based on a superhuman effort at self-understanding or self-realization.

In Mahayana understanding, insights into the true nature of self and phenomena are wordless; they are intuitive truths. This is how the Mahayana tradition understood prajna-wisdom: cognition without words. This understanding plays itself out in the famous dictum, many centuries later in China, of Bodhidharma, the founding ancestor of Zen tradition:

a special transmission outside the scriptures [i.e., textual
   knowledge]
without depending on words and letters
pointing directly to one's own mind
seeing into one's true nature and realizing buddhahood

The Heart Sutra is a guide to how cognition or realization should be understood. In such cognition there is nothing concretized to point to. There is no "attainment"—if attainment is understood in terms such as climbing Mount Everest or swimming across the English Channel or memorizing the entire Encyclopedia Britannica. At the same time, all claims of "spiritual attainment" have to be seen as manifestations of ego structures.

Another point of contention with regard to the problem of "attainment" in the Heart Sutra formulations seems to have centered around the problem of defining a model of awakening or enlightenment. Soon after the death of the Buddha, a controversy emerged over the status of the arahat, the model of a saint in early texts; at the Second Council (held about a hundred years after the death of the Buddha) one of the key issues was whether it was possible for an arahat to relapse. The dissenting monks, who were to become the nucleus of a movement that would become, centuries later, the Mahayana, argued for an alternate model of sainthood which became known as the bodhisattva model. The mature articulations of this new model argued for perceiving all things, including spiritual attainment, as having provisional nature. Anything that can be apprehended by senses, including suffering and its ending, is a psychological construct—and thus is fundamentally empty of intrinsic existence; any "attainment" is likewise a construct. These arguments from ancient India for the provisional nature of all constructs correspond quite well to the orientation of contemporary postmodern philosophy which rejects all absolutes of any kind.

The bodhisattva depends on Prajna Paramita, and the mind is no hindrance; without any hindrance, no fears exist. Far apart from any perverted view, one dwells in Nirvana.

Instead of the arahat model of the earlier tradition, the Prajna Paramita sutras—and the Heart Sutra—are champions of the new paradigm of the bodhisattva. The Mahayana innovation was to argue that the bodhisattva can be male or female, monastic or lay. The bodhisattva is steadfast in his or her trust in the wisdom of shunyata rather than the textuality of Abhidhamma scholasticism or even of the four noble truths as she works her way toward awakening. In this paradigm it is not so much that the four noble truths are ignored or rejected as that they are simply not given the same *a priori* sanctity that the orthodox tradition seemed to assign to them. The four noble truths or any other teaching of the Buddha cannot be, in this reckoning, "holy" simply because the Buddha had spoken them. Any teaching is validated only when it is verified and found to be viable in one's own experience.

The Sanskrit phrase for "mind is no hindrance" is *viharaty acitta-varanah*, which literally translates as "dwells (*viharaty*) without (*a-*) mind's (*citta*) barriers (*avaranah*)." Edward Conze translates "mind's barriers" as "thought-coverings." He says that the word *avarana*, from the root *vri*, means "obstruction," "obstacle," "impediment," or "covering."[31] He goes on to say that the Buddhist tradition distinguishes three types of hindrances: karmic, defilement-based, and cognitive. Karmic hindrances comprise those residuals of past unwholesome actions that continue to seed the consciousness in unexamined ways. The defilement-based hindrances consist of those fueled by greed, hatred, delusion, and so forth. The third, cognitive hindrances include those that result from belief in things existing separately from the observing consciousness.

Conze says that "the term used here, *citta-avarana*, is very rare, and I assume it to be identical with the third kind of obstacles, the cognitive ones. Some manuscripts of the Hridaya read 'Thought-object' (*citta-alambana*) instead."[32]

These words thus seem to reinforce the argument of the Heart Sutra, namely, that the real problem in human conditioning is a misperception and miscognition of the nature of phenomena, driven by currently generated defilements seeded by past defilements. Many of these ideas in the Heart Sutra were to become building blocks for a later development in Buddhist psychology that came to be called Yogachara Buddhism in early medieval India.

The bodhisattva finds in prajna a sense of completion and is completely at peace with it and with herself. The prajna-wisdom is her support; through a deep understanding of the paradox of an ultimate lack of svabhava in things, she has the realization that there is nothing lacking anywhere. Whatever the limitations of her conditioned mind may be, she has a perfect understanding of, and trust in, the wisdom of shunyata. No perverted or deluded views cloud her vision.

In traditional Buddhism, there are "four perverted views" from which liberation is sought:

the view that anything existent can be permanent even if it is compounded

the view that satisfaction may be found in the world of compounded entities

the view that there is an abiding, permanent core, a self or soul

the view that because things are attractive, they are worth striving for and clinging to (the Pali tradition renders this as "seeing the lovely in the unlovely")

The Pali word for "perverted views" is *vipallasa*, and it is perhaps better translated as "deluded views" or even "distortions." It is perhaps appropriate to point out that of all the teachings of the Buddha, those

on delusion are the most compelling and the most original. These teachings separate the Buddha from all other religious and philosophical
thinkers not only in his own time but also in subsequent generations.

An investment in any of these "perverted" views is likely to produce
fear and confusion. Fear and confusion, by their very nature, seek out
things to cling to, and each clinging brings about its own particular perverted view to further cloud the vision. Rooted firmly in the wisdom of
shunyata, the bodhisattva has no such hindrance. She does not mistake
the unreal for the real, the conditioned for the unconditioned, the rela-
tive for the absolute.

The basic teaching of the Buddha is that the mind is originally
uncontaminated. There is no concept of original sin in Buddhism.
Defilements accrue to the mind but they do not inhere. This is the basis
of Buddha's teaching of nirvana, of liberation, of awakening, all of
which are a "recovery" of what was already there rather than the acquir-
ing of something new.

Hindrances or defilements are "filters" that individuals accrue as a
result of conditioning during development from infancy to childhood
to adolescence to adulthood. The Buddha's teaching is that behind all
the accumulated filters the mind remains essentially untainted. The
metaphor here is a mirror. A dirty mirror, when cleaned, shines. In the
same way, when all the conditioning filters have been removed by a
trust in the prajna-wisdom, in shunyata, the mind recovers its original
joyfulness, and hindrances and fears have no place to take hold. For a
contemporary reader of the sutra, the words "no fears exist" may be
one of its most significant teachings. The horrors of the twentieth century, and the way humans have treated one another, have produced
extraordinary anxiety, despair, and hopelessness. Today we are gripped
by all kinds of insecurities. Individuals find their lives driven by fears
of various kinds even while they yearn for love. Our conditioning has
become so convoluted that we not only fear fear itself but also fear
intimacy.

In our complex society today, any hope for transformation of the individual as well as the collective must deal with the basic fear of duality, fear of the "other," fear of a world that is threatening yet indispensable. Unless this sense of separation from the world is resolved, all our efforts to find meaning in life will be nothing more than manipulative gestures. Through the wisdom understanding of shunyata one can transcend the manipulative gestures that the social consensus, in its ignorance, sees not as illusions but as solid truths. The training of the bodhisattva is to see the illusory nature of all facets of our conditioning and transcend them.

With a clear mind and an unclouded vision, the bodhisattva "dwells in nirvana." For the earliest custodians of Buddhist tradition, the Sthavira monks, nirvana was an experience of liberation, the sense of relief and freedom that comes when one has eliminated all craving, clinging, and notions of permanent selfhood. The resulting condition, in which all layers of stress have been dispelled, was the "end of suffering."

As happened with many of the Buddha's teachings, nirvana too came to be posited as a categorical imperative—a thing-in-itself—in the Abhidhamma schema. It became an existent outside human psychological experience. Innumerable difficulties have been caused by a misreading of a single passage in the Pali suttas that speaks of nirvana as the unconditioned:

> There is, bhikkhus, a not-born, a not-brought-to-being, a not-made, a not-conditioned. If, bhikkhus, there were no not-born, not-brought-to-being, not-made, not-conditioned, no escape would be discerned from what is born, brought-to-being, made, conditioned. But since there is a not-born, a not-brought-to-being, a not-made, a not-conditioned, therefore an escape is discerned from what is born, brought-to-being, made, conditioned.[33]

Any number of Buddhist teachers have interpreted words such as "unconditioned," "deathless," and "nirvana" as the nouns they seem to be, thus creating hermeneutical difficulties. But the problem has also been compounded by passages from the Abhidhamma that say: "Great Seers who are free from craving declare that Nibbana is an objective state which is deathless, absolutely endless, unconditioned, and unsurpassed."[34]

It is not clear whether, in these early debates among Buddhists in ancient India, the protagonists were truly aware of the implications of claims about an "objective state." Such claims lead to ontological reifications, which a trained Buddhist thinker would hardly be expected to engage in. Even if they were aware of what they were claiming, they might not have been aware of the consequences of their linguistic constructions. But regardless of whether these claims were ontologically deficient or just linguistically flawed, they created substantive problems.

The Mahayana response to the "nouning" of nirvana was to espouse a "verbing" position and deny nirvana as a transcendental thing-in-itself. Their argument was that a fear of samsara cannot be the same thing as, say, a fear of a snake about to strike your leg. Samsara is a conceptual construct, and therefore a fear of it is equally psychological and subjective. If a fear of samsara is self-created and self-imposed, its resolution in nirvana is equally self-created. Thus, by definition, nirvana is nothing more than an overcoming of the (self-imposed) fear of samsara, and not a thing-in-itself. In this understanding both samsara and nirvana are processes, thereby making the "attaining" of nirvana an impossibility. According to Mahayana thinkers, seeking to overcome the fear of samsara by finding a refuge in nirvana is a dualistic approach and cannot lead to transcendent wisdom, which is essentially nondualistic and in which samsara and nirvana are not distinct. Nirvana is not to be considered "a thing," a category existing as a reality apart from everything else; samsara, likewise, is not an entity existing apart from everything else.

Nirvana is not the result of doing something or attaining something, but of *not-doing*, which means not engaging in unskillful behaviors of thought, speech, and action. The bodhisattva does not "attain" nirvana (since any attainment is empty of temporal duration or self-nature), but his vision is unclouded through nondiscrimination. In other words, through the prajna-wisdom of shunyata, the bodhisattva is always contented and at peace with how phenomena manifest themselves.

In this sense, nirvana is best understood as *upekkha* (equanimity). Bhikku Bodhi, an outstanding translator of Pali texts today, offers this nuanced understanding of *upekkha*:

> The Buddha used a term of rare occurrence in the pre-Buddhist languages in India, namely, *upekkha* (Skt. *upeksha*, a word formed out of *upa* + *iks*, meaning "taking a close look"). It is generally rendered into English as "equanimity," a term of more ethical import, but which highlights the epistemological stance, hence better translated as "consideration." This is because a prejudiced mind, a mind that has already been made up, cannot consider anything that is contrary to its accepted views. Hence, a "considering mind" beautifully defined as one which has become pliable (*kammaniya*), become stable (*thita*), become flexible (*mudubhuta*) and reached a state of not fluttering (*anenjapatta*). This is a concentrated mind (*samahita*), without blemish (*anagana*), purified (*parisuddha*) and cleansed (*pariyodata*) with all defiling tendencies gone (*vigatu-pakkilesa*). It is almost difficult to think of the salutary effects of adopting such a perspective in the investigative processes relating to science, technology, medicine, economics, political science and sociology to mention a few. This is especially so in the context of the modern world where all such disciplines are based upon the inflexible and rigid dichotomies such as the true and false, the existent and the non-existent. Absolutism of some sort is the inevitable result.
>
> The good and the peaceful that he attained under the Bodhi tree permeated all his teachings, whether they pertain to explanations of the physical or objective world, the human personality, social, political and moral life as well as the use of the most important method of communication, namely, language.[35]

George Leonard, who was introduced earlier as one of the founders of the Human Potential Movement in the 1960s and 1970s, has used the secular, experiential term "crystalline state" to speak of a state of being that resonates with the definition of upekkha above:

In the crystalline state, there is no expectation over any prejudgment. Concentration on the past and future gives way to primary focus on the present. Action taken while in the crystalline state is not considered action but rather *appropriate action*. When fully achieved, this state permits awareness of the perfect rhythm that always exists at the heart of your being. Going into the crystalline state does not require a set of instructions; it can come upon you spontaneously... Likewise, no set of instructions can assure that you will achieve this state.[36]

Within the context of the Heart Sutra, a conflation of upeksha with nirvana permeates classical Mahayana understanding of nirvana. In this conflation, nirvana is shunyata because it has no graspable nature, any thought of nirvana as an attainable object would therefore be an error. Nirvana is not something to be striven for but to be seen as a natural resultant from its predicate, cessation (*nirodha*), which deconstructs all the structures of defilements and hindrances. The experiential status of nirvana is to be intuited in the unfolding of each moment where shunyata plays itself out unceasingly. Through his intuitive wisdom, prajna, the bodhisattva knows that in shunyata all things are just as they really are, that is, full of thusness or suchness (*tathata*) in their manifestation.

Thus, a proper understanding of the line "Far apart from any perverted view, one dwells in nirvana" may be "Far apart from any perverted view, one dwells in upeksha." This alternate reading seems to be much more in line with the spirit of the sutra.

In the three worlds all buddhas depend on Prajna Paramita and attain Anuttara Samyak Sambodhi.

The "three worlds" are the worlds of past, present, and future (at times also interpreted as the worlds of form, formlessness, and desire). In these three worlds or time periods the transcendental wisdom of shunyata is the vehicle that enables aspiring buddhas to complete their liberation project. In the Indian Mahayana tradition it is taken for granted that an aspiring bodhisattva is synonymous with an aspiring buddha, since a bodhisattva is aspiring for buddhahood.

Anuttara Samyak Sambodhi means "Perfect Unexcelled Awakening." It is the enlightenment of a perfect buddha (*sambuddha*), one who has by him- or herself rediscovered the wisdom that leads to liberation. In traditional Mahayana usage, Anuttara Samyak Sambodhi is also a statement about the completion of the bodhisattva path, that is, the realization of buddhahood. Such buddhahood puts one in possession of the "ten powers" (Skt: *dashabala*) of a Perfect Buddha:

knowledge of discernment in any situation of what's possible and what's not

knowledge of ripening of deeds in oneself and others

knowledge of superior and inferior abilities of other beings

knowledge of tendencies in other beings

knowledge of the manifold constituents of the world

knowledge of paths leading to rebirth in various realms of existence

knowledge of what will lead to purity and what to impurity

knowledge of various meditations (*dhyana*) and concentrations (*samadhi*)

knowledge of death and rebirth

knowledge of when the defilements are completely eradicated

The "attainment" of these ten powers in Anuttara Samyak Sambodhi may seem, on the surface, a logical contradiction since the sutra has just declared that there is "no attainment" and "nothing to attain." The implicit message here is that in and of itself Anuttara Samyak Sambodhi too is empty, but the ten powers arising out of completing the path can be used as skillful means, which, along with wisdom and compassion, is the hallmark of a bodhisattva in the Mahayana literature. Possessing these ten powers, the bodhisattva works tirelessly to save all beings knowing fully well that all is inherently empty. The effort is directed toward helping individuals change their karmic legacies and patterns rather than saving any solidity called a being.

Anuttara Samyak Sambodhi changes the complexion of the sutra from a mere rejection of Abhidhamma categories to a positive fulfillment of the bodhisattva vow to save or liberate all beings, "All beings, one body; I vow to liberate." The bodhisattva treads on this path immersed in the intuitive wisdom of shunyata rather than in the rational categories of Abhidhamma or in the illusion that there is someone who can "save" someone.

The wisdom of shunyata is not an opinion or a category but a realization in the bones and the marrow of the practitioner; it is a realization of the empty nature of phenomena rolling on endlessly, in which the practitioner does not see herself or himself as intrinsically separated from the rest of the phenomenal world. In this way of cognizing phenomena, the experiencer and the experienced are inseparable and indistinguishable. The bodhisattva and those being "saved" are also inseparable from one another.

Therefore, know that Prajna Paramita is the great transcendent mantra, is the great bright mantra, is the utmost mantra, is the supreme mantra, which is able to relieve all suffering and is true, not false.

Here the sutra's celebration of insight into shunyata comes to an end. Historically, however, by the time the Heart Sutra was given its final shape, the influence of *mantrayana* (the vehicle or modality of mantra practice) and Tantra (collections of secret, esoteric texts and ritual practices) was clearly ascendant within the Mahayana. Thus the exhortation in the Heart Sutra to the listener from now on is to be seen in its historical context as an addendum of a proselytizing nature. The assertions made here clearly contradict the insights presented earlier in the sutra.

Commentators throughout ages have taken differing positions on the inclusion of the mantra in the sutra. Perhaps the best way to sum up the mantra's place is to note its historical context and leave its use entirely up to the reader—whether as an incantation, as a tool of psychic power, or whatever. Certainly, the myths and legends associated with the life and adventures of Xuanzang will lean toward the magical and the miraculous. A more discerning inquirer may see the mantra as almost a kind of "sound-based theology" within the Buddhist traditions of early medieval India at a time when devotionalism was also making its mark on the broader Indian culture and Hinduism. Or it may be seen as a linguistic and symbolic summation of the central teaching of Mahayana wisdom schools.

A distinction should perhaps be made here between a *mantra* and a *dharani*. A *mantra* is usually a string of unintelligible syllables, while a *dharani* is considered to be an intelligent summary of some profound truth. In some folk-tradition practices, however, dharanis may be strings of unintelligible syllables. Korean folk Buddhism, for instance, is full of such dharanis; here it is more the norm than an exception that the entire

Heart Sutra will be used as a dharani. Such usage perhaps follows the protocols of Chinese folk Buddhism, within which the entire sutra was used by Xuanzang as a dharani during his dangerous crossing of the Taklamakan desert. In Tibetan Buddhism, it is more common to repeat the mantra as a focused practice. In sum, because of its brevity, the Heart Sutra lends itself to being practiced easily either as a dharani or as a mantra.

As should be clear from earlier comments, one of the hopes in this modern commentary on an ancient text is to show a continuity of collaborations and boundary-crossings in earlier generations so that today we are dealing not only with the taxonomy of the text itself but also with its historical usages. As one of the "house texts" (despite its well-known anti-intellectualism, the institutional Zen adopted certain texts for purposes of chanting or memorized learning; among them are the Heart Sutra, the Diamond Sutra, and the Lankavatara Sutra) of the Zen tradition, the Heart Sutra has seen itself appropriated, sometime directly, other times indirectly, for various forays of all shapes and varieties by Zen masters in China, Japan, and Korea. Earlier, we saw how Xuanzang's chanting of the Heart Sutra as a dharani during his dangerous desert crossing solidified its status as a magical spell in popular Chinese imagination. An equally significant development took place in early Sung China (960–1279) when one of the minor schools of Chinese Zen, the Fayan school, founded by Fayan Wenyi (885–958) morphed into a collaboration of Zen and Pure Land practices. Fayan is best known today as the teacher differentiating between "moon" (i.e., enlightenment) and "finger pointing to the moon" (i.e., teaching leading to enlightenment); the collaboration was actually brought into effect by his grand-disciple Yongming Yanshou (905–975)who was later proclaimed the first patriarch of the Pure Land school by the Sung emperor.

Because the Fayan school was short-lived in China itself, the impact of its collaboration with Pure Land was not noticeable in the country of its origin but "Fayan Zen" became quite influential in Korea in later centuries. As a result, today's Zen "practice" in Korea covers a spectrum in which devotional practices, chanting of mantra, prostrations, and so on intermingle with the classical practice of formal, upright sitting posture.

This spectrum, thus, crosses boundaries between formal Zen sitting practice and mantra chanting in the same way that the Heart Sutra text does between doctrinal sophistication and mantra chanting. There's a similar spectrum in Tibetan Buddhism, with the result that an inclusion of a mantra at the end of the Heart Sutra is neither surprising nor unexpected to a person well-versed in East Asian Buddhism or Tibetan Buddhism.

A positive view of this mantra is offered by Thich Nhat Hanh, a contemporary Vietnamese Zen master:

> When we listen to this mantra, we should bring ourselves into that state of attention, of concentration, so that we can receive the strength emanated by Avalokiteshvara Bodhisattva. We do not recite the Heart Sutra like singing a song, or with our intellect alone. If you practice the meditation on emptiness, if you penetrate the nature of interbeing with all your heart, your body, and your mind, you will realize a state that is quite concentrated. If you say the mantra then, with all your being, the mantra will have power and you will be able to have real communication, real communion with Avalokiteshvara, and you will be able to transform yourself in the direction of enlightenment. This text is not just for chanting, or to be put on an altar for worship. It is given to us as a tool to work for our liberation, for the liberation of all beings.[37]

Clearly the message of these lines of the Heart Sutra is intended for the unconvinced and the uninitiated. It asks for faith and trust in the efficacy of the sutra (a hallmark of Mahayana methods of veneration) rather than the critical-analytical faculty of self-investigation (the Abhidhamma approach). A faith in the power of the mantra is a further development within the Mahayana and is reflective of the growing popularity of the Lotus Sutra (*Saddharma-pundarika Sutra*) and sutras from the

Pure Land schools. These sutras belong to a category distinct from the Prajna Paramita sutras, but they much more easily crossed cultural boundaries into China and East Asia to become objects of devotion and blessing-seeking than was the case in Indian Mahayana, which remained much more philosophical. The time of the composition of the Heart Sutra also coincides with the rise of Tantra within Indian Buddhism. These internal developments, combined with external pressures on Indian Buddhist missionaries, were to become dominant in China, Japan, and Korea. The success of these missionaries was to change the very nature of Indian Mahayana, at times into an unrecognizable shape.

The magico-mantric culture that these Buddhist missionaries brought with them found receptive soil in the countries of North and East Asia and led to tremendous religious and sociocultural realignments in these lands. To cite just one example, even today in the Japanese Shingon sect of Buddhism novice monks chant the Heart Sutra while standing under an icy waterfall to induce a catatonic spell. One contemporary scholar, Michael Pye, has argued that this use of the Heart Sutra as a mantra/spell only confirms the presence of a wide variety of tools used by Buddhist practitioners in their practice (as opposed to philosophers debating the finer points of doctrine). He writes:

Mahayana Buddhism in Sanskrit form had both meaningless spells and meaningful ones. Meaningless ones may be found, for example, in the Dharani chapter of the Lotus Sutra. Once transliterated into Chinese and Japanese all Sanskrit words lose their meaning, not only spells. On the other hand if used sufficiently frequently in understood contexts, they maintain and develop their meaning. For example, although many Japanese might have difficulty in expounding it, the word *hannya* (*Prajna*) is not strictly speaking meaningless in Japanese. When it comes to a mantra the interpretative tradition is complicated by the importance attachment to the power of the syllables themselves in this "tantric" phase of Buddhism. But such an adaptation of the old Brahmanical tradition that special syllables such as *OM* or *A* were able to sum up all truth as utterances of power, did not prevent the syllables from being allegorically interpreted as well... Given this general character of Buddhism it is not particularly surprising that the Heart Sutra is used in the context of ascetic exercises such as the Buddha himself gave up (or never even started, in the case of standing under the waterfalls), the attainment of trance states which count as falling short of enlightenment or nirvana, exorcisms of malignant spirits which in reality are a delusion, and healings which leave the body just as prone to disease, old age and death as it ever was before.[38]

Michael Pye seems to point to a consistent feature in folk Buddhism in all Asian societies where many Buddhist texts or excerpts were used as justification for or accessorizing ascetic practices for the sake of healing or exorcism. The Buddha expressly forbade his monks to engage in these practices and asked them to focus instead on their own awakening. Since very few monks were able to come to the same kind of awakening that the historical Buddha had come to, many monks embraced the ambiguous territory between Buddhist teachings (essentially a pursuit of insight and wisdom) and shamanism (essentially a pursuit of the magical and the occult). It is a matter of anthropological interest and record that many of the practices at the folk level that are considered "Buddhist" are essentially shamanic practices. The Heart Sutra has been adopted over and over again by these folk aspects of Asian Buddhism and used as a spell for healing or getting into trance states. At the same time, its philosophical acuity has continued to attract scholars and thinkers.

So proclaim the Prajna Paramita mantra, proclaim the mantra which says: "Gate, gate, paragate, parasamgate, bodhi svaha."

Gate, gate (pronounced *ga-tay ga-tay*) means "gone, gone"; *para* means "beyond"; *para-gate* means "gone beyond"; *para-sam-gate* means "gone completely beyond [to the other shore of samsara, the sea of suffering]"; *bodhi* means the Awakened Mind; *svaha* is the Sanskrit word for homage or proclamation. Thus the entire mantra means "Homage to the Awakened Mind which has gone over to the other shore."

The critical word here is "beyond," which may also be translated as "transcendent" in a careful contextualization. As has been mentioned above, an iconic understanding of samsara in the Buddhist tradition has been "a sea of suffering." Within this understanding, there is "this shore" and the "other shore." "This shore" is the realm of samsara, a place of suffering resulting from a conglomeration of one's karmic conditions and predilections in the present life. The "other shore" or the "far shore" is the nirvanic realm representing a resolution of those karmic conditions, through whatever methodology, and is a place of ease and tranquility, of refuge and safety. This other shore is "beyond" samsara, a transcendence of the psychological afflictions.

In the early tradition, the teachings of the Buddha were seen as a raft that transports one from this shore to the other shore. In this metaphor, samsara is likened to a river and the raft carries one to the other shore of the river. In Mahayana articulations, the six *paramitas* (perfections, or virtuous cultivations) of generosity, ethical discipline, patience, wholesome effort, meditation, and wisdom are seen as the raft that takes a practitioner across the sea of suffering. In this understanding, wisdom or prajna is at times seen as the container in which the other five *paramitas* are nestled; hence the primacy of wisdom (of shunyata) as the raft that leads to liberation.

Whatever perspective one takes on the mantra that closes the sutra,

there can be no dispute that the text has multiple facets: the radical negation of Abhidhamma categories; the positive assertion of the bodhisattva's striving for buddhahood, and the mantric practice that's more
folk than doctrinal. To this construct add later developments in the
Indo-Tibetan tradition where the Heart Sutra became the basis for esoteric visualization practices of Tantra-based Vajrayana Buddhism.[39]

As was mentioned in the introductory chapter, the challenge for contemporary readers of the Heart Sutra is whether to align themselves
primarily with what the sutra has tried to convey prior to the mantra—
namely, rich insight and intuitive wisdom coming from a completely
still mind, layers of stress brought to complete cessation, and a knowing consciousness transcending all concepts and categories. In this vein,
it is also possible to see the mantra itself as an homage to a consciousness grounded in upeksha, the equipoise of tranquility and serenity
whose essential stillness is not disturbed by the arising and passing away
of phenomena.

By contrast, the reader also has the option of stepping into the folk traditions of the Heart Sutra with their long histories in China, Japan, and
Korea, as well as Tibet, and to see its mantric orientation as inclining it
more toward the magical and the mystical. A positive understanding of
shunyata, within these esoteric practices, can emerge if it is seen that all
artificial layers of selfhood and ego are sacrificed in the compassionate
presence of Avalokiteshvara. Such sacrifice/surrender can ideally generate an insight into both shunyata and the lack of a stable, permanent self.

Those Zen masters who are willing and able to guide their students
toward the theme of shunyata, especially within the context of the Heart
Sutra, find in it perhaps a resonance of the existentialist theme that life
has no inherent meaning or reason. "Life" and "meaning" are linguistic-
conceptual constructs that can find validation only within their own cir-
cular logic. Within the framework of shunyata teaching, as captured in
the Heart Sutra, any understanding of meaning has to confront the problem of svabhava—own-being or an abiding, unchanging core.

The Heart Sutra uses negation to point to this lack of any inherent meaning or reason in the phenomenal world, including the world of conceptual thinking. It takes each of the existents, holds it in an unflinching gaze, and declares it to have no sustaining self-nature. This is the radical wisdom of shunyata in the Mahayana tradition.

Compassion is the other, equally crucial element in Mahayana teachings. How do we then bridge the gap between shunyata as the ultimate nature of things and the conventionality of the human condition? The existentialist thinkers of the twentieth century agonized over this problem and were led to despair and anarchy. In Mahayana frameworks, compassion is a natural, unforced by-product of a deep state of meditation; it supports the wisdom of emptiness. It allows the individual to have empathy with the conventional appearance of the world without getting lost in it. It may be that compassion works best as a post-enlightenment existential response, but cultivation of compassion can also be a gentle smoothing of one's practice to be skillfully applied whenever one gets lost in the conventionalities of the world. Regardless, without compassion as a guiding paradigm, the unrelenting precision of shunyata can make living unbearable.

Zen masters insist that our true freedom lies in the choices we make, not in our conceptual constructs, faith, or beliefs. Each of us has the power to change the despair inherent in (the conceptual construct of) "no meaning" into the living vitality of "Great Meaning"—to change "no reason" into "Great Reason." In this understanding, meaning is derived from action, not from conceptual thinking. If the action is kind, generous, and compassionate—and backed up by the core intention of kindness, generosity, and compassion—that's all that matters.

The argument is that in a state of deep meditation one accesses the core psychological qualities of kindness and compassion. There's also a co-emergent insight that all beings are also naturally endowed with the same qualities.

We lose this natural quality whenever we hold ourselves separate from everything else. In the language of the Mahayana, this separation is a devaluation of the self and the world; to see others as separate from oneself is to live in delusion and deny one's own buddha-nature; to see others as sharing in one's own buddha-nature is to affirm one's own essential humanity. In making a free choice of compassion for all beings, we are doing no more than giving expression to our buddha-nature. It is only in compassion (*karuna*) that wisdom (*prajna*) finds its fullest expression.

This way of understanding the Heart Sutra in Zen and Mahayana traditions may be presented as a circle:

180 degrees
experience of complete stillness and
cessation; nirvana; shunyata

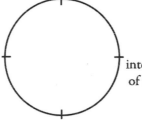

270 degrees
attainment of the ten
powers of Anuttara
Samyak Sambodhi;
time and space
are no hindrance

90 degrees
dry cognition;
intellectual apprehension
of the causes of suffering

0 degrees
turning the Wheel of Samsara/Karma through greed, hatred, and delusion
is also
360 degrees
turning the Wheel of Dharma through compassion and wisdom;
seeing things just as they are

0 **degrees**. This is samsara. Here the Wheel of Karma keeps turning, fueled by greed, anger, and delusion. An urgency to change, to get out of the realm of suffering leads one to...

90 **degrees**. Here one has an intellectual awareness of the four noble truths and the chain of dependent origination, but this is a "dry" cognition. When this dry cognition is supplemented with a deepening experience of meditation, one reaches...

180 **degrees**. Here one has a taste of complete stillness, of the empty nature of phenomena; one experiences cessation of the working of greed, hatred, and delusion. When the mind becomes completely silent all personal and societal conditioning disappears. In Zen terms this is the realization of one's "original self," a recovery of the uncontaminated conditioning with which one was born. A continued and thorough absorption in this stillness leads to...

270 **degrees**. Here one may acquire the ten powers of Anuttara Samyak Sambodhi as a by-product of one's absorption in the highly concentrated meditation or samadhi practice. This is the attainment of buddhahood in the traditional Buddhist sense. It is also the place where magic and psychic powers may become a playground of the adept. At the same time one understands, through one's wisdom-eye, that these powers too are empty. This wisdom leads to...

360 **degrees**. This is nirvana in action, or buddhahood manifested through functioning in the world. Here the Wheel of Dharma (which is none other than the Wheel of Karma turning in reverse) is turned by employing skillful means rooted in wisdom and compassion. Here one finds validation of one's bodhisattva vows, a continuation of what Shakyamuni Buddha achieved in his forty-five years of teaching.

I first learned the above "Zen Circle" from my teacher, the Korean Zen master Seung Sahn (1927–2004), as part of his oral teachings. It has since been included in his book, *The Compass of Zen*. (The interpretation above, however, is entirely my own and I take responsibility for its shortcomings.)

More than two centuries ago Voltaire wrote, "Man makes his own gods, forges forever new chains for himself." Today we live in a post-religious society; our psychological and spiritual needs have evolved and have arguably transcended the making of gods and the forging of new chains. Our need today is to find a paradigm in which the intellectual and the intuitive can meet, a paradigm that is rooted in the wisdom of our meditative experience. Today researchers in the field of conscious-ness studies use terms like "holographic" to describe a new model of the universe in which an individual is a "hologram" and exists in a state of "holonomy."

> The idea of the universe as an overachieving unity repeated some-how in each of its parts bears a majesty and elegance all its own... The holonomic formulation... resonates with one of the most ancient intuitions of the race, expressed with eloquence and force in Eastern philosophy. It helps account for the essential meaning-fulness of existence, the coherent, repeated patterns that we keep discovering at the deepest structure of language, mathematics, and the physical world. It is a necessary consequence of modern quan-tum theory taken to its logical extreme.[40]

The holographic model of the universe cannot be replicated in indi-viduals by turning it into yet another ideology or manipulative societal realignment. Without a thorough realization of shunyata, which allows us to get in touch with our basic humanity, "holonomy" will be just another concept, the subject of disputations and dissertations. But the paradigms created by Mahayana thinkers and the findings of quantum theory can both bring us, in our experience of deep meditation, to "a world of connectedness, potential, and evolution" in which we turn toward a vivid sense of community along with the acceptance of personal responsibility; toward a de-emphasis on competing and winning along with a re-emphasis on participating and experiencing; from aggression toward gentleness and enjoyment; from dominance of nature to blending with nature; from exponential growth in production and consumption to a more moderate, more ecological standard of living along with a powerful intentionality; toward social justice throughout the world.[41]

Compare this to the sentiments expressed by the contemporary Zen master Thich Nhat Hanh:

The Prajnaparamita gives us a solid ground to making peace with ourselves, for transcending the fear of birth and death, the duality of this and that. In the light of emptiness, everything is everything else, we inter-are; everyone is responsible for everything that happens in life. When you produce peace and happiness in yourself, with the conscious breathing that you produce in yourself, you begin to work for peace in the world. To smile is not to smile only for yourself; the world will change because of your smile. When you practice sitting meditation, if you enjoy even one moment of your sitting, if you establish serenity and happiness inside yourself, you provide the world with a solid base of practice. If you do not give yourself peace, how can you share it with others?[42]

Appendix:
A Re-rendering of the Great Heart
of Perfect Wisdom Sutra

This free-form rendering of the Heart Sutra is both playful and serious: playful in the sense that it takes liberties with interpreting Sanskrit words in ways that do not always correspond to etymological protocols; serious in the sense that it is trying to recapture the intention behind what was written in the original Sanskrit version hundreds of years ago. It seems to me that it is possible to unpack the language of the original text just a little bit without losing the vitality of its creative insights.

The Great Heart of Perfect Wisdom Sutra

Avalokiteshvara Bodhisattva, while dwelling in the far-reaching depths of her meditation, perceives that [when a practitioner has a realization that] the constituent dharmas of five skandhas have no own-being, he is protected from all anguish and distress.

Shariputra, a form carries its own trace of shunyata, the ultimate lack; shunyata, the ultimate lack, is traced back only through form. That which is form is a reflection of shunyata, its ultimate lack; that which is shunyata, ultimate lack, is intuited only in form. The same is true of the skandhas called sensations, perceptions, formation, and consciousness.

Shariputra, all constituent dharmas carry a trace of their lack of own-being. Things lacking in own-being do not appear or disappear, are not tainted or pure, do not increase or decrease. Therefore, in radical shunyata there are no own-being-bearing forms, no own-being-bearing sensations, perceptions, impulses, and consciousness. Also there are no own-being-bearing eighteen composites of consciousness: no eyes, no ears, no nose, no tongue, no body, no mind, no color, no sound, no smell, no taste, no touch, no object of mind, no realm of eyes, and so forth until no realm of mind consciousness. Also there are no own-being-bearing links of dependent origination: no ignorance and also no extinction of it, and so forth until no old age and death. Also there is no own-being-bearing extinction of them in nirvana.

There are no own-being-bearing four noble truths either; no own-being-bearing suffering; no own-being-bearing origination; no own-being-bearing stopping; no path; no cognition; also no attainment of nirvana with nothing to attain.

The bodhisattva depends on Prajna-shunyata, and the conditioned mind is no hindrance. Without any hindrance, there are no fears for the turbulence of samsara. Far apart from any distortions of perceptions and views, one dwells in the unshakable peace of no-construction.

In the three worlds, all buddhas depend on Prajna-shunyata and go deeper into the cultivation of Anuttara Samyak Sambodhi, the Perfect Unexcelled Awakening, as skillful means.

Therefore know that Prajna-shunyata is the great transcendent refuge, is the great bright refuge, is the utmost refuge, is the supreme refuge which is able to relieve all anguish and distress, and does not fail its practitioner.

So enter the Prajna-shunyata, enter the refuge that is the space of

Gate, gate, paragate, parasamgate, bodhi svaha.

Gone; gone; gone beyond; gone beyond all forms and contingent becomings; the awakened mind, homage.

Notes

1. Leonard, *Silent Pulse*, p. xii.
2. Capra, *Tao of Physics*, pp. 197–98.
3. Conze, *Buddhist Wisdom Books*, p. 18.
4. Dumoulin, *Zen Buddhism*, p. 35.
5. Jan Nattier, "The Heart Sutra: A Chinese Apocryphal Text?" *Journal of the International Association of Buddhist Studies* 15, no. 2 (1992).
6. Dumoulin, *Zen Buddhism*, p. 35.
7. Edward Conze, quoted in Lopez, *Heart Sutra Explained*, p. 3.
8. Waddell, *Zen Words for the Heart*, p. 31.
9. Lopez, *Heart Sutra Explained*, p. 7.
10. Mu Soeng, "How Deep (and Sad) Is Your Love?" *Buddhadharma Quarterly*, Fall 2007.
11. Chun-fang Yu, *Kuan Yin: The Chinese Transformation of Avalokiteshvara* (New York: Columbia University Press, 2001).
12. Richard H. Robinson and Willard L. Johnson, *Buddhist Religion: A Historical Introduction*, 4th ed. (Belmont, CA: Wadsworth, 1997), p. 86.
13. Ibid., p. 86.
14. Ibid., p. 87.
15. Leonard, *Silent Pulse*, pp. 32–34.
16. Jack Kornfield, "The Smile of the Buddha," in *Ancient Wisdom and Modern Science*, ed. Stanislav Grof (Albany: State University of New York Press, 1984), p. 101.
17. Leonard, *Silent Pulse*, p. 176.
18. See Fritjof Capra, "The New Vision of Reality," in Grof, *Ancient Wisdom*, p. 138.
19. Ibid.
20. Capra, *Tao of Physics*, pp. 198–99.
21. Chang, *Buddhist Teaching of Totality*, pp. 60–61.
22. Abe, *Zen and Western Thought*, p. 94.
23. Govinda, *Creative Meditation*, p. 11.

24. Ibid., pp. 60–61.

25. W. H. Auden, "Canzone."

26. Pine, *Heart Sutra*, p. 59.

27. Kazuaki Tanahashi, ed., *Moon in a Dewdrop* (San Francisco: North Point, 1985), p. 70.

28. Seung Sahn, *Compass of Zen*, private printing at Providence Zen Center.

29. Robert Buswell, ed., *The Korean Approach to Zen: The Collected Works of Chinul* (Honolulu: University of Hawaii Press, 1983), pp. 146–47.

30. Werner Heisenberg, quoted in Capra, "New Vision of Reality," p. 137.

31. Conze, *Buddhist Wisdom Books*, p. 95.

32. Ibid.

33. Ireland, *The Udana and the Itivuttaka*, p. 103.

34. Bhikkhu Bodhi, trans., *A Comprehensive Manual of Abhidhamma* (Seattle: BPS Pariyatti Edition, 2000), p. 260.

35. Bhikkhu Bodhi, "Uniqueness of the Buddha's Doctrine," *Buddhist Publication Society Newsletter*, no. 48 (2001).

36. Leonard, *Silent Pulse*, p. 173 (italics in the original).

37. Nhat Hanh, *Heart of Understanding*, pp. 50–51.

38. Michael Pye, *The Heart Sutra in Japanese Context*, in *Prajnaparamita and Related Systems: Studies in Honor of Edward Conze*, ed. Lewis Lancaster (Berkeley: University of California Press, 1977), pp. 128, 130.

39. An interested reader is directed to Lopez, *Elaborations on Emptiness*, pp. 116–40, which includes descriptions of these highly complex—and eso-teric—visualization practices.

40. Leonard, *Silent Pulse*, p. 89

41. Ibid., p. 177.

42. Nhat Hanh, *Heart of Understanding*, pp. 51–52.

Bibliography

Abe, Masao. *Zen and Western Thought*. Honolulu: University of Hawaii Press, 1985.

Capra, Fritjof. *The Tao of Physics*. Boston: Shambhala, 1976.

Chang, Garma C. C. *Buddhist Teaching of Totality*. University Park: Pennsylvania State University Press, 1971.

Conze, Edward. *Buddhism: Its Essence and Development*. New York: Harper and Row, 1975.

———. *Buddhist Thought in India*. Ann Arbor: University of Michigan Press, 1967.

———. *Buddhist Wisdom Books*. New York: Harper and Row, 1972.

———. *Selected Sayings from the Perfection of Wisdom*, Boulder, CO: Prajna Press, 1978.

———. *Thirty Years of Buddhist Studies*. Columbia: University of South Carolina Press, 1968.

Dumoulin, Heinrich. *Zen Buddhism: A History*. Vol. 1. New York: Macmillan, 1968.

Fox, Douglas. *The Heart of Buddhist Wisdom*. Lewiston, NY: Edwin Mellen, 1985.

Govinda, Lama Anagarika. *Creative Meditation and Multi-Dimensional Consciousness*. Wheaton, IL: Theosophical Publishing House, 1976.

Grof, Stanislav, ed. *Ancient Wisdom and Modern Science*. Albany: State University of New York Press, 1984.

Gyatso, Geshe Kelsang. *Heart of Wisdom: A Commentary to the Heart Sutra*. London: Tharpa Publications, 1986.

Ireland, John D., trans. *The Udana and the Itivuttaka*. Kandy, Sri Lanka: Buddhist Publication Society, 1997.

Kenney, Jim. "Particle, Wave, and Paradox." In *Fireball and the Lotus*, ed. Ron Miller and Jim Kenney. Santa Fe: Bear, 1987.

Khenpo, Palden Sherab. *Ceaseless Echoes of the Great Silence*. Boca Raton, FL: Sky Dancer, 1993.

Kothari, D. S. "Atom and the Self." In *The Evolution of Consciousness*, ed. Kishore Gandhi. New York: Paragon House, 1983.

Leonard, George. *The Silent Pulse*. New York: E. P. Dutton, 1978.

Lopez, Donald, Jr. *Elaborations on Emptiness: Uses of the Heart Sutra*. Princeton, NJ: Princeton University Press, 1996.

——. *The Heart Sutra Explained*. Albany: State University of New York Press, 1988.

Murti, T. R. V. *The Central Philosophy of Buddhism*. London: George Allen & Unwin, 1955.

Nhat Hanh, Thich. *The Heart of Understanding*. Berkeley, Parallax, 1988.

Pine, Red (Bill Porter). *The Heart Sutra: The Womb of Buddhas*. Washington, DC: Shoemaker & Hoard, 2004.

Streng, Frederick. *Emptiness: A Study in Religious Meaning*. Nashville, TN: Abingdon, 1977.

Talbot, Michael. *Mysticism and the New Physics*. New York: Bantam, 1980.

Waddell, Norman. *Zen Words for the Heart: Hakuin's Commentary on the Heart Sutra*. Boston: Shambhala, 1996.

Wallace, B. Alan. *Choosing Reality: A Contemplative View of Physics and the Mind*. Boston: Shambhala, 1989.

Acknowledgments

Acknowledgment is made to the following for their kind permission to use materials from their publications:

Selections from *The Tao of Physics* ©1975 Fritjof Capra. Reprinted by permission of the publisher.

Selections from *The Silent Pulse* ©1978 George Leonard. Reprinted by permission of the author.

Selections from *Creative Meditation and Multi-Dimensional Consciousness* ©1976 Lama Anagarika Govinda. Reprinted by permission of the publisher.

Selections from *The Buddhist Teaching of Totality* ©1971 The Pennsylvania State University Press. Reprinted by permission of the publisher.

Selections from *Ancient Wisdom and Modern Science* ©1984 State University of New York Press. Reprinted by permission of the publisher.

Selections from *The Heart of Understanding* ©1988 Thich Nhat Hanh. Reprinted by permission of the publisher.

Index

About the Author

Mu Soeng is well known to Buddhist pracitioners, particularly within the Insight Meditation community. He is the program director and teacher of Mahayana Buddhism at the Barre Center for Buddhist Studies in Barre, Massachusetts, and the author of the highly acclaimed *The Diamond Sutra: Transforming the Way We Perceive the World* and *Trust in Mind: The Rebellion of Chinese Zen*.

About Wisdom

Wisdom Publications, a nonprofit publisher, is dedicated to making available authentic works relating to Buddhism for the benefit of all. We publish books by ancient and modern masters in all traditions of Buddhism, translations of important texts, and original scholarship. Additionally, we offer books that explore East-West themes unfolding as traditional Buddhism encounters our modern culture in all its aspects. Our titles are published with the appreciation of Buddhism as a living philosophy, and with the special commitment to preserve and transmit important works from Buddhism's many traditions.

To learn more about Wisdom, or to browse books online, visit our website at www.wisdompubs.org.

You may request a copy of our catalog online or by writing to this address:

Wisdom Publications
199 Elm Street
Somerville, Massachusetts 02144 USA
Telephone: 617-776-7416
Fax: 617-776-7841
Email: info@wisdompubs.org
www.wisdompubs.org

The Wisdom Trust

As a nonprofit publisher, Wisdom is dedicated to the publication of Dharma books for the benefit of all sentient beings and dependent upon the kindness and generosity of sponsors in order to do so. If you would like to make a donation to Wisdom, you may do so through our website or our Somerville office. If you would like to help sponsor the publication of a book, please write or email us at the address above.

Thank you.

Wisdom is a nonprofit, charitable 501(c)(3) organization affiliated with the Foundation for the Preservation of the Mahayana Tradition (FPMT).